I0418251

GOD'S
PROMISES

GOD'S
PROMISES

A PRAYER JOURNAL

Pastor Rick
Stephenson

God's Promises: A Prayer Journal
Copyright © 2022 Rick Stephenson

Unless otherwise indicated, all scriptural quotations are taken from
The Holy Bible, King James Version, Copyright © 1994 by Zondervan
Publishing House, Grand Rapids, MI. All rights reserved.

Scripture quotations marked MSG are taken from The Message: The
Bible in Contemporary Language, Copyright © 2021 Peterson, Eugene
H., NavPress.

Unless otherwise indicated, all dictionary definitions are taken from
"Dictionary.com Is the World's Favorite Online Dictionary." © 2022
Dictionary.com, Dictionary.com, **https://www.dictionary.com/browse**.

Paperback ISBN: 979-8-9858122-3-7

Cover Design: 99Designs.com
Page Design & Layout: LucyHoltsnider.com
Editor: Mandi Summit – Red Quill Co LLC

All rights reserved. No part of this publication may be reproduced,
distributed, or transmitted in any form or by any means, electronic
or mechanical, including photocopying and recording, or by any
information storage and retrieval system without the prior written
permission of the publisher, except in the case of brief quotations
embodied in critical reviews and certain other noncommercial uses
permitted by copyright law.

Although the author and publisher have made every effort to ensure
that the information in this publication was correct at press time, the
author and publisher do not assume and hereby disclaim any liability
to any party for any loss, damage, or disruption caused by errors or
omissions, whether such errors or omissions result from negligence,
accident, or any other cause. Any perceived slight of any individual or
organization is purely unintentional.

For more information, email **Rick-Stephenson@wisdomwell.guru**.

A FREE GIFT FOR YOU!

Subscribe to the newsletter and receive a free booklet!

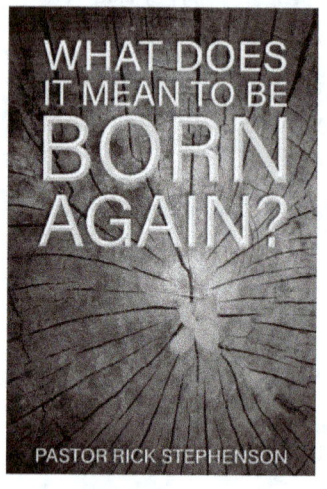

Have you ever wondered what Jesus meant when he said, "You must be born again," as found in the Gospel of John? You've likely heard many interpretations of this scripture, and it's a good idea to make sure for yourself that you have indeed been born again according to the manner in which God intended.

Remove all doubt by reading this brief contemporary and easy-to-comprehend booklet, by Pastor Rick Stephenson. In this conversational and relatable booklet, Pastor Rick walks you through the true Biblical meaning behind what it means to be born again.

You Will Learn:
- **How Jesus's words of spiritual birth are related to physical birth.**
- **The extensive process God uses for bringing about new birth in a believer.**
- **The exclusive proof that validates the new birth experience has happened to you.**
- **What is expected of a believer once they have been born again.**

Understanding the words of Jesus will move you into a deeper, more meaningful relationship with God and allow you to experience the new birth in a full, enriching, and rewarding manner.

Begin the journey to discover what it means to be born again by reading this amazing booklet now!
Sign up today by visiting
www.WisdomWell.guru\newsletter

LIVE THE ABUNDANT LIFE GOD PROMISED YOU!

You've been living for God and pursuing the abundant life He promised you in scripture, but you're not having nearly the success you expected and you want to know why. Or maybe you don't know God and you simply want the most satisfying life you can possibly have, but you're not sure what that entails. In this conversational and relevant book, Pastor Rick Stephenson presents the answers to an abundant life.

You Will Learn:
- **Why we struggle to obtain abundance.**
- **What true abundance looks like from God's point of view.**
- **What God's promise of an abundant life requires of us.**
- **How to establish a proper core from which to emanate abundance.**
- **How to maintain abundance once obtained.**

Understanding the concepts in this book will open the door to your abundant life by removing the stress and worry from your pursuit. It truly is up to you, and you can achieve it by keeping one thing in mind: you need to *Exercise Your M.I.G.H.T.*!

**Get started living the abundant life God
promised you today!
Order your copy today at
www.WisdomWell.guru\products**

One day he was praying in a certain place. When

he finished, one of his disciples said, Master,

teach us to pray just as John taught his disciples.

So he said, When you pray, say,

Father,

Reveal who you are.

Set the world right.

Keep us alive with three square meals.

Keep us forgiven with you and forgiving others.

Keep us safe from ourselves and the Devil.

Here's what I'm saying:

Ask and you'll get;

Seek and you'll find;

Knock and the door will open.

Don't bargain with God. Be direct.

Ask for what you need.

Luke 11:1–4 & 9–10 (MSG)

THIS PRAYER JOURNAL BELONGS TO:

*Name:*_____

Address: _____

City, State & Zip _____

*Phone:*_____

*E-Mail*_____

**So let God work his will in you.
Yell a loud no to the Devil and watch him scamper.
Say a quiet yes to God and he'll be there in no time.
Quit dabbling in sin. Purify your inner life.
Quit playing the field.
Hit bottom, and cry your eyes out.
The fun and games are over.
Get serious, really serious. Get down on your knees
before the Master; it's the only way
you'll get on your feet.**

James 4:7-10 (MSG)

DEDICATION

This prayer journal is dedicated to all the pastors, ministers, family and friends in my life who have helped teach me to pray. Moreover, I want to thank all those who have prayed for and with me, especially in the difficult times when I couldn't find the words to pray myself.

You've all helped me understand that prayer is simply our way of communicating to God. You've demonstrated that it should come from our heart and we should pray in such a way as though God were right there with us and we were merely talking with our best friend.

I value these prayerful lessons more than you will ever know.

CONTENTS

INTRODUCTION

Thank you for picking up this prayer journal. With that one small action, you are on your way to more meaningful interaction and devotional time with God. I believe anyone who has a desire to connect with our Great Creator will be blessed because of their time spent in prayer.

> *He is a rewarder of them that diligently seek him.*
> (Hebrews 11:6b)

Don't worry if you are new to prayer. This journal is meant to help guide you on your journey to a place where you feel more comfortable with the concept of prayer and to assist you in growing your relationship with God.

At the end of this brief study, you will find several lined pages to use as a convenient place to make notes as you go along. The note pages are followed by daily journal pages specifically structured in such a way for you to capture several details regarding your prayer time and habits. The daily journal pages are laid out in such a way as to assist you in identifying your particular prayer trends. By knowing what your preferred prayer environment consists of and how God tends to speak to you, you can then make your prayer time more meaningful and purposeful, which in turn can lead to greater intimacy with God.

You can be as detailed as you like in the journal, choosing to track such things as time of day, setting, who you prayed for, situations you prayed about, personal requests made to God, etc. Remember to come back and follow up with pertinent details such as specific answers God provided regarding your prayers, any scriptures that came to your mind, or experiences you had during your day that confirmed God's existence and love.

These pages are meant to be flexible and provide space to document your journey with God, so use them however you see fit. The point is to experiment and see what works best for you. Use the pages to help you avoid monotony in your prayer time. My recommendation would be to try your best to document as much as you can daily, and then at the end of each week, review your journal and search for patterns, trends, and confirmations. Doing this over time will help to solidify the fact that God does indeed answer your prayers and work in your life. I believe you will also be amazed at the results!

Draw nigh to God, and he will draw nigh to you. (James 4:8)

WHY A PRAYER JOURNAL?

Pure and simple, this prayer journal is to encourage you to pray. We all need encouragement every now and again, especially in the area of prayer.

I believe prayer is vital to growing in our faith and our relationship with God. It's the means of communicating directly with our Creator who is eagerly waiting to hear from us. It's a manner in which we can address our needs and concerns directly with the One who can actually do something about them.

Understand that prayer doesn't change God, but it can influence how He responds to us. Just read this example from King Hezekiah's experience:

> *In those days was Hezekiah sick unto death. And the prophet Isaiah the son of Amoz came to him, and said unto him, Thus saith the Lord, Set thine house in order; for thou shalt die, and not live. <u>Then he turned his face to the wall, and prayed unto the Lord,</u> saying, I beseech thee, O Lord, remember now how I have walked before thee in truth and with a perfect heart, and have done that which is good in thy sight. And Hezekiah wept sore. And it came to pass, afore Isaiah was gone out into the middle court, that the word of the Lord came to him, saying, Turn again, and tell Hezekiah the captain of my people, Thus saith the Lord, the God of David thy father, <u>I have heard thy prayer,</u> I have seen thy tears: behold, I will heal thee: on the third day thou shalt go up unto the house of the Lord. And I will add unto thy days fifteen years; and I will deliver thee and this city out of the hand of the king of Assyria; and I will defend this city for mine own sake, and for my servant David's sake.*
> (2 Kings 20:1–6) (Emphasis mine.)

However, prayer isn't just a tool to influence God to work on our behalf. In fact, if we're honest with ourselves, this rarely happens, because quite plainly, God is God. He can decide what to do all on His own without us. But isn't it nice to know He takes what we have to say under consideration?

Prayer is more about how it changes *us*. Through prayer, the answers we receive and the connection we make with God, we learn and grow as a result, which develops our character and shapes us to become more like Him. Becoming more like Christ is really the ultimate goal of the Christian, isn't it? Then to do so, we must communicate or pray regularly.

This prayer journal is not intended to be a complete study of prayer, but rather a highlight of some aspects to inspire you to participate in regular communion with God. Therefore, it's my hope that you will find some effective reminders as to what prayer is about, why it's important, discover basics on how to begin praying, and even learn some prayer patterns you can customize to develop a more meaningful, richer, and fuller prayer life.

I decided to add a journal element because it is important to record your prayer experiences. As human beings, we tend to be forgetful. Therefore by writing things down, we can come back to them as often as we need to. This is called memorializing and God is big on creating memorials—specific instances where, when and how God moved for us to come back to see and remember Him. Memorials strengthen our bond to the one being remembered.

And the Lord said unto Moses, Write this for a memorial in a book, and rehearse it in the ears of Joshua.
(Exodus 17:14a)

What types of things could you document? How about a prayer list? Write down the things you intend to pray for, the answers received, and the specific things that God tells you personally in prayer, because as you will experience, prayer is a two-way street. We talk and He listens, He talks, and it is then that *we* are supposed to listen. (We'll talk further about listening to God as a part of your prayer time in another section.)

You can view this journaling process as a prayer experiment. Try documenting your prayer times for a period of 30 days and then take note of the trends, such as the time of day you prayed, the amount of time spent in prayer, and the types of prayers that tend to work best for you. I believe that if you are faithful to this for 30 days, you will find that your prayer life has developed into something you value and don't want to give up or miss.

I suggest 30 days here because most behavior experts indicate that it takes at least 21 days to establish a habit (simply Google how to start a new habit and you'll see what I mean). There is also something called the 21/90 rule. In order to establish a new habit, you need to be consistent with it for 21 days, then afterward continue for another 90 days so that it becomes a permanent lifestyle change. With all of this information, I suggest you start with 30 days to firmly establish your prayer habit, and I believe if you do, you will be self-motivated to continue and make prayer part of your daily lifestyle.

PRAYER DEFINED

To begin, I believe we need a good working definition of prayer. What does it mean to pray? If it were tangible, what would it feel like, look like, smell like, taste like, etc.? Therefore, we need some descriptors for prayer. As a starting point, when you look up the word prayer in the dictionary (www.dictionary.com), several definitions pop up, but the three that stood out to me are:

a) a spiritual communion with God or an object of worship, as in supplication, thanksgiving, adoration, or confession

b) a negligible hope or chance (e.g., Do you *think he has a prayer of getting that job?)*

c) a formula or sequence of words used in or appointed for praying (e.g., the Lord's Prayer)

Using the dictionary definitions, we need to break them down to make them more relevant to our study. Let's begin by examining the first definition of prayer, "a spiritual communion with God or an object of worship." There are some words we need to further understand—such as spiritual, communion, God or an object, and worship—in order to fully grasp the meaning.

WHAT DOES IT MEAN TO BE SPIRITUAL?

According to the dictionary, to be spiritual means that there is a focus on aspects which relate to the soul or spirit in contrast to material things. It also means that a connection is established by an affinity (similarity in structure or attraction) of the mind, spirit, or temperament. Hence, if we are going to be spiritual, we should tap into (or develop a similar structure or attraction to) the larger Spirit, and as scripture indicates, this would be God Himself.

> *God is a Spirit: and they that worship him must worship him in spirit and in truth.*
> (John 4:24)

Many will claim they are spiritual, but their actions don't reflect it. Being spiritual is different from being religious. Being religious simply means we are following a set of rites or rituals. Rites and rituals come from a place of routine, and for the most part can be performed with little to no thought. As such, there's no real effort to complete those tasks.

Being spiritual, however, means we must engage and participate on a mental level. We need to think clearly about what we are doing and why we are doing it, connecting action with purpose. In addition, being spiritual requires us to be true to ourself as well.

Consider the age-old question, "How are you?" The ritual in us replies automatically and regardless of truth, "I'm fine." In contrast, if we approached this question on a spiritual level, we would pause for a moment and consider the words, the environment, the one asking, and how we are truly feeling. Only once all those aspects have been considered would we respond, and then it would be an honest response.

Therefore, being spiritual requires our mental capacity. In human terms, our spirit is connected to our mind, emotions, attitude, and ways of behaving or energy expended. Some may also refer to this as our heart. Therefore, when we hear the phrase, "Give your heart to God," it is inferred that all our thoughts, feelings, motivations, and energy should be given to Him.

And he answering said, Thou shalt love the Lord thy God with all thy heart, and with all thy soul, and with all thy strength, and with all thy mind; and thy neighbour as thyself.
(Luke 10:27)

To accomplish this complete giving of ourself to God, prayer should be a time of little to no distractions whenever possible. I understand that life seems to keep getting busier and busier, but please do not put off praying simply because you can't avoid distractions. God desires that we communicate with Him no matter what our circumstances might be. Ultimately, whether we are distraction free or not, we should set our minds and energy on making a connection with God during our time of prayer. But whenever possible, we'll find the experience of prayer much more satisfying when we have limited our distractions.

A COMMUNION CONCERN

Communion is a feeling of emotional closeness or intimacy. It's a relationship connection in which deep thoughts and feelings are shared without fear of judgment, ridicule, or rejection. In other words, prayer should be a time in which we can completely open up to God without being fearful that He will ignore or criticize us.

If you went to your best friend who is your absolute confidant and shared your closely held secrets and emotions, only to discover that friend betrayed you by letting these things be known to others, would you share with them again? I don't think you would, and the word would quickly spread that this person could not be trusted.

For thousands of years now, the fact that God can be trusted has spread across all the nations and peoples of the globe. I think it's a given that He can keep our secrets and treat our innermost thoughts and feelings with ultimate care and concern. Isn't it amazing that we can trust Him without any doubt?

Communion is only felt by those who are willing to be vulnerable. We can't establish meaningful relationships by keeping everything to ourself. We have to share with those we want to be close with, disclosing warts and all—the good, the bad and the ugly, as they say. We take the risk for communion because we know that the reward is intimacy with another person, and often the baring of vulnerabilities is reciprocated. Not only do we learn about the other person, but we discover things about ourself as well—things that we may not have touched on before.

When we are vulnerable and honest with God in our prayers, we will find ourself changed by prayer. We will discover things that God already knows about us, but that we have been too blind to acknowledge. We will also begin to learn things about God that take us to a deeper place with Him as He shows us more of who He really is.

Understand that God already knows us on a very intimate level. After all, He formed and fashioned each of us in our mother's womb before we even took in our first breath.

> *For thou hast possessed my reins: thou hast covered me in my mother's womb. I will praise thee; for I am fearfully and wonderfully made: marvellous are thy works; and that my soul knoweth right well. My substance was not hid from thee, when I was made in secret, and curiously wrought in the lowest parts of the earth. Thine eyes did see my substance, yet being*

unperfect; and in thy book all my members were
written, which in continuance were fashioned, when
as yet there was none of them.
(Psalm 139:13–16)

Although He knows everything there is to know about us, still He longs for a deep level of communication that can only come when we actively participate and get to know ourself. As we do so, our walls will come down and we will be more willing to share and enter the sacred space of communion.

GOD OR AN OBJECT

Prayer is meant to be directed toward someone or something. However, when I understand that prayer is being directed at a lifeless object, I get a little concerned. Objects are inanimate—they can't hear, see, or speak. When we bow before a statue, that's an inanimate object. How can we expect a response from marble, stone or concrete? There is no life in those things.

One might try to justify it by saying those statues represent the one they're praying to. But then, why not just pray? Why bow before these objects?

What about praying to living things? Even though plants, trees, and animals are alive, they are not exactly like us. Therefore, how can they relate to us? We may even stroke our pet's head and talk to them as if they know what we are saying, but deep down we know there is still something missing in the connection. As scripture points out, this is not the case with God.

So God created man in his own image, in the image of
God created he him; male and female created he them.
(Genesis 1:27)

We have been made in the image of God and in His likeness. He even took it one-step further and became like one of us in the form of Jesus. He wanted to relate to us on a deeper level. Therefore, if our prayer is going to be scriptural, we are directed to send our prayers to God alone, not another human being who is filled with faults and flaws like ourself.

> *In the beginning was the Word, and the Word was*
> *with God, and the Word was God....*
> *And the Word was made flesh, and dwelt among*
> *us, and we beheld his glory, the glory as of the only*
> *begotten of the Father, full of grace and truth.*
> (John 1:1 & 14)

Hence, when choosing to pray, it is best to choose to direct those prayers to God, who is the only one who can do anything about our prayers anyway.

I'd like to share a personal story that shows the power of prayer to the true God. I was having some knee pain that the doctors just couldn't address. They were unable tell me the reason for the pain I was feeling, so lacking a solid understanding, they suggested a knee brace. I tried it out, but it didn't give me any relief. Finally, I thought to ask God to heal me of it.

I prayed about it before trying to go up a set of stairs at work. In that moment, I still felt pain in my knee, but I reminded myself to remain faithful. I had prayed about it and now it was up to God. Later that day, I had to use that same set of stairs, only this time, I noticed my knee no longer hurt. Miraculously, I haven't had an issue with my knee ever since. It took my faith and prayer to bring it to pass and this is the power of directing our prayers to God.

AN ELEMENT OF WORSHIP

Prayer should also contain an element of worship. If we have agreed that God should be the recipient of our prayers, then worship in prayer makes sense, since worship is described as treating somebody or something as a deity.

More than that, worship means to love somebody deeply and to admire and respect them greatly. Isn't God, the Creator of the Universe and King over all, worthy of our admiration and respect? Especially when we consider the fact that this incredibly powerful and all-knowing entity is willing to stop and listen to what His lowly creation has to tell Him. In fact, He's eagerly waiting and longing to hear from us.

Therefore, our prayer should include worshipping God as a way to express our love and enable growth in our relationship with Him. Because He first showed us such love by being willing to lay down His life for our redemption, shouldn't we in turn show him our love? We can do this by communicating with Him and sharing intimate information to create deeper bonds of closeness and love. Love only grows when it is expressed because it exposes areas in which we can grow. When we tell someone we love them and why, it reveals other areas in which we may be lacking in love, thereby affording us an opportunity to address it.

IT NEEDS TO BE OUT LOUD

I used to belong to a church affiliation that would encourage believers to pray during the service. The head of the service would say to the congregation, "Let's pray," and complete silence would follow, where it was assumed that everyone was praying silently.

I often wondered about the silence, curious if this time was really considered by God to be prayer. I am sure I'm not alone in having often found my thoughts traveling down several highways of concerns, imaginations, and things to get done once the silence and service was over. Additionally, years of talking with others who have told me they often like to pray quietly to themselves made me wonder who they were really praying to so silently.

Is this the way God truly likes us to pray? I believe the answer is a resounding no! I believe God intended prayer to be an audible verbal exchange, and in this section, I'll explain why.

God gave man free will when He created Adam and Eve. Free will is often interchangeable with the phrase "power of choice." In other words, when God placed man in the Garden of Eden along with both the trees of life and of knowledge of good and evil, He allowed man to make a choice all on his own. There was no fence, no barricade, and no hindrance to either tree. There was only a simple ordinance from God.

> *Of every tree of the garden thou mayest freely eat:*
> *But of the tree of the knowledge of good and evil,*
> *thou shalt not eat of it: for in the day that thou eatest*
> *thereof thou shalt surely die.*
> (Genesis 2:15–17)

So, there it was, the first choice laid out before them to either obey or not. I'm positive thoughts immediately began running through their minds as to what each tree could offer. What would be the impact if they chose one over the other? As Adam and Eve were perusing through this new field of thought, along came the serpent, or as we know him, the devil. Satan took their lack of understanding of God as an opportunity to introduce new thoughts into their minds.

Here's an important factor to consider—did simply having these thoughts condemn Adam and Eve to the punishment God had laid out? No, it did not, and what a relief that is! So, what did determine that Adam and Eve should be punished? It came about because of their action—the moment they ate of that which God had instructed them not to.

Throughout the day, we get bombarded with both good and bad thoughts. If God were to act on our thoughts alone, most of us would never have made it past puberty. Instead, we would be a smoldering heap of ash somewhere in the hallways of our high school. Therefore, isn't it wonderful that God uses something other than our thoughts alone to move on our behalf?

What does He use then to move in our life? Words. Our spoken words to be exact. When we speak, we have made a choice to take the thoughts we think and express them. It is an exercise of our free will when we speak aloud. Through this expression of free will, we give God permission to move in our lives through our prayers. Because of this, I believe that prayer should be said aloud as a form of commitment to our thoughts.

Countless times in scripture, especially in the book of Exodus, God says that He has heard the cry of His people and is responding accordingly. Yet nowhere in scripture do we find that He was acting in response to only knowing their thoughts. And while Jesus questioned the thoughts of some, he did not act in fulfillment of those thoughts alone. Even God chose to express His communication with us through tongues (Acts 2) rather than some ESP mind game.

Therefore, if we are going to pray, it must be out loud, otherwise it is called meditation. Now, don't get me wrong—I'm not suggesting that meditation isn't valuable. We also need times of quiet reflection to organize our thoughts and pray effectively, and that's where meditation comes in. Meditation is the concentration of the mind and the act of thinking about something carefully, calmly, and for some time. After meditating we can then pray out loud making an obvious commitment to what we are praying about. In reality, we need both meditation and prayer to communicate fully and wholeheartedly with God.

> _**Let the words of my mouth**, and the **meditation of my heart**, be acceptable in thy sight, O LORD, my strength, and my redeemer.**_
> (Psalm 19:14) (Emphasis mine.)

So, meditate when you need to reflect, and pray out loud when you've determined what you are praying for. Of course the volume of that prayer is up to you. It could range anywhere from a mere whisper to a boisterous shout, whichever you desire in that moment, and whichever will benefit you the most when expressing yourself to God.

WHY IS IT SO DIFFICULT?

At times, it can be difficult to make ourself pray or to know what to pray about.

Why is praying so hard sometimes? I'm not sure I have an answer to that question. The only thing that comes to mind is that there is constantly a war going on between the flesh and the spirit. The spirit wants to pray and do what is right, but the flesh wants to please only itself.

> *Watch and pray, that ye enter not into temptation: the spirit indeed is willing, but the flesh is weak.*
> (Matthew 26:41)

It is not always comfortable to kneel or humble ourselves and ask for help. We tend to think of asking for help as a sign of weakness, and being prideful, it goes against our natural tendencies to do so. Therefore, we must discipline our body and conform it to adhere to a routine of prayer. I don't mean a routine in the sense of saying the same prayers repeatedly, but rather trying to establish a set time and place to pray, which is another purpose for this prayer journal. Additionally, we need to discipline ourselves to feel comfortable praying out loud, which only comes through practice. Hence, the more we pray, the easier it becomes.

As far as knowing *what* to pray about, that can be difficult, too. Sometimes we may think that what we are praying about doesn't register high enough on the importance meter for God to even address it, but this is just a tactic of the enemy to keep us from praying. Satan knows that prayer connects us to God and he doesn't want us to experience or strengthen that connection. When we feel that connection, we want more of it and we pursue it with greater gusto. Rather than questioning if what we are praying about is worthy enough, let's focus on understanding that God loves to connect with us even in the smallest details of our lives because it builds intimacy.

Let's look at a tangible example of why we routinely ask our spouse or significant other at the end of the day how their day was. We usually get the same responses day after day, don't we? Sure, there a few minor differences in the highlights here or there, but if their job is routine, we know we're going to pretty much get the same story night after night, so why even ask? We do it because we have a genuine interest in our spouse as a person and because it builds our intimacy with them.

It's the same with our relationship with God. We can take every care and concern to Him in prayer because He *wants* to hear from us. He's waiting to hear from us, even if it's just a quick hello.

Casting all your care upon him; for he careth for you.
(1 Peter 5:7)

HELP IN GETTING STARTED

There are many ways to get started in prayer and I have outlined several in another section of this journal to help you find some focus when you pray. However, the best advice I can give you is the old Nike slogan, "Just do it!"

Make yourself pray!

Set a time and place to pray. Mix it up and determine what works best for you. Perhaps morning is the only available time in your schedule. A lunch break could also work well, or maybe you can only find time at night after the kids go to bed. Any combination of these could work also if you need to break it into smaller chunks of time.

You may also need to find motivations that work for you to remind you to pray. It could be either a poster, a slogan, a printed Bible verse, or even an alarm that encourages you to pray. Personally, I am a fan of Post-it Notes. Just look in my office and you'll see that they are everywhere. I've attached them to my computer screen, keyboard, desk, books, even notepads. (Yes, I know that seems silly, but I really do have Post-it Notes on my notepads.) Without them, I am afraid I will forget something. I know I need the help where I can get it, as I believe most of us do. So, they are here and there and everywhere with reminders of the things I need to do or accomplish.

For me, it's Post-it notes. You will need to find whatever works for *you*. Try and experiment until you do, and simply be faithful to the time of day and motivations you choose. With prayer, you will soon find the excess reminders are no longer necessary because the deep personal relationship you share with your Maker will be motivation enough. That's the purpose of this prayer journal—to help you figure out a routine that works for you. If you have already figured it out, then this journal will help you fine-tune it.

TYPES OF PRAYER

There are many types of prayers—prayers of repentance, thanksgiving, protection, provision, rejoicing, petition, and so on. So, how do we know what is the right prayer? It's whichever one addresses our current need at the time. Our need is usually tied to our emotion of the moment.

Remember, we are made in God's image. We are emotional beings, which means He must be emotional as well. God understands our emotions and He designed prayer as a way for us to express them directly to Him. Our emotions often drive our choices and so they will drive the types of prayers we offer.

Look at the example of a car dealership. Just walk into a car dealership and if you are not careful, you may drive out with the car that caught your eye or rather your emotions. Car sales are primarily driven on emotional responses. This is simply an example to reflect that our needs are usually tied into our emotions and our emotions may be tied into our physical or spiritual state, since they are the go between for the two.

Also, a friend of mine pointed out that we are not all tempted by the same car. One may be intrigued by the sleek sports car but someone else may be lured by the snazzy new truck. While we all have the same emotions, we don't all have the same expression of those emotions. The expression of our emotions is tied to who we are as a person, the spirit within us. And this is why it is best to pray in your own words rather than repeating someone else's prayer.

PRAY WITHOUT CEASING

The Bible encourages us to:

> *Pray without ceasing.*
> (1 Thessalonians 5:17)

What does this really mean? It means that we should live in a state of constant communication with God. That's not to say we need to be praying aloud nonstop, but we should feel free to pray anytime and anywhere—no matter if it's in the shower, the car, at a restaurant, at church, or even at work. Anytime we want to communicate with our best friend, what do we do? We pause and place a quick phone call, text, or email. It should be the same when we want to communicate with God. We should stop what we are doing and send out a quick prayer. A simple "I love you, Jesus" here and there throughout the day or a "Lord, please give me wisdom for this meeting I'm about to attend." Whatever, whenever—that's the bottom line.

I believe the idea of praying without ceasing extends to our children. We shouldn't neglect the importance of teaching prayer to our children. Teach them how to pray as well as the importance of prayer. In this manner, our legacy of prayer will continue and won't end with us. Just as Jesus encouraged the children to come to him so they could experience his touch and interaction, we need to lead by example and encourage our children to seek God.

> *But Jesus said, Suffer little children, and forbid them not, to come unto me: for of such is the kingdom of heaven.*
> (Matthew 19:14)

GOD'S PROMISES

Why does the title of this prayer journal include the phrase "God's Promises"? Because one aspect of prayer is often recognizing, praying, and holding God accountable to the promises He made to us in His word. God *wants* us to claim His promises, however as the word "promise" implies, it is a two-way agreement. In other words, God will do His part *if we do ours.*

Allow me to share my friend's childhood Sunday school story to illustrate this. One day, two little girls were walking to school together when they realized they were going to be late. One decided she would stop to pray about it, while the other decided to pray as she ran toward the school. Who do you think made it to school on time?

Prayer can help us identify how or what we need to address, and it's important that we do our part once we realize what it is. By praying, we allow God to speak into our life about areas in which we need to act. It also provides an opportunity for us to remind God to fulfill His side of the promise. Not that God truly needs reminding, but our words allow Him to see the level of our desire as we plead our case and seek His movement in our lives.

Once we've done our part, we need to be aware of what God's part entails and be observant as to how He answers, just like the following illustration.

A man was sailing when his boat struck a rock. It started to sink until he ended up treading water. The whole time, he was praying to God to be saved. Soon, a boat came by and offered to help, but he waved it off saying God was going to help him. Shortly after, an ocean liner passed by and offered to bring him to shore, but he didn't get on board, saying again that God would save him. Finally, a rescue helicopter flew overhead, but he refused their assistance as well, insisting God would save him. Eventually, the man got so tired of treading water that he drowned.

When he reached heaven, the man was confused and asked God why he didn't help him. "I sent help three times," God said, pointing out the boat, the ocean liner, and the helicopter. The man had been so focused on expecting a miraculous event—like the parting of the Red Sea or deliverance by a whale like Jonah—that he had missed the obvious.

While it is natural for God to be supernatural and to provide miraculous answers to our prayers, we also need to realize that sometimes the answers to our prayers come in very common or subtle ways. Unfortunately, because this is often the case, we rarely end up giving God proper credit. My hope is that this journal will help you recognize how God moves in your life and to encourage you to praise Him no matter how your answers arrive.

The overall benefit to praying for God's promises is that God's word will be embedded so deeply into our being that in times of need, we will have access to internal reminders, which will in turn provide us more strength and faith to continue to trust in God. As you establish your own prayer time, be sure to read the scripture and pray it back to God in your own words, then ask that He complete His promises in your life—and be sure to do *your* part!

A NEGLIGIBLE HOPE
(NOT A CHANCE)

The term negligible according to the dictionary means insignificant—too small or unimportant to be worth considering. A negligible hope, therefore, basically means there is an incredibly slim chance of something happening or getting better. While this definition of prayer is meant to explain a concept where the problem or difficulty is so big that even prayer may not help, I feel that the dictionary has it backwards. Rather than prayer being a negligible hope, I believe if someone prays, the *problems and difficulties* they face become negligible. I've come to this conclusion from personal experience—the answers God gives are not always the ones I want, but He answers all the same. The biggest factor here is that God hears me and answers my prayers, and He'll do the same for you.

Prayer works! How do we know? Because we can see in scripture that God answers the prayers of those who seek Him. Further evidence exists in the generations and generations of people who have turned to God in prayer to obtain answers, direction, and the encouragement they need. God turned their moments of trouble into triumph. If prayer were not a successful means to petition our Creator, word would have spread like wildfire long ago to put out the flames of intercession. However, over time the exact opposite has occurred. Isn't it exciting to know that someone out there cares enough to listen to us and respond?

I could share several stories about how God answered my own prayers, like healing me when I needed it, providing financially when all my resources were gone, or guiding me to a job that allowed me to not only provide a living but to minister to others the precious word of God, however I want to make this lesson about prayer as concise as I can, so let me simply state again—prayer works!

The premise and purpose of this prayer journal is to learn how to make prayer work for you. It will be up to you to establish a routine and utilize prayer to witness God's promises being fulfilled in your own life. It doesn't take much to begin—just willingness and a little self-discipline—and I trust that this brief study and journal will help you do just that. I want to encourage your willingness to build the discipline you need to reap the rewards of a devoted and personally satisfying relationship with our Lord and Savior.

For prayer to work, simply tell God what is on your mind, how you are feeling, and what concerns you have. He is waiting to communicate with you and He is always listening. So, what are you waiting for? Jump in and get started today! Begin building your communion with God and discover just how prayer can work to enrich your life.

BE SURE TO LISTEN

Anytime you spend your energy in prayer, be sure to take some time to listen for God's response. Remember prayer is meant to be communication with God, and communication requires two parties to interact with each other. If all we do is talk to God about our needs, dreams, and desires, but we never listen to His response, then we have not truly communicated. Instead, all we have done is lectured Him. We need to listen in order to hear what God has to say about the things we've expressed to Him, or even for things we may not have mentioned.

How does God speak to us? Well, there are numerous ways and I don't want to limit God nor his ability to reach us. For most, it's a small quiet voice they feel in their head or heart. It's not usually audible, although it could be at times. For others, it's an impression or a thought. It may be a sign or a confirmation of something that occurs that speaks to us. The point is to quiet yourself for a moment and ask God to respond. I believe it's in that response that we will know beyond a shadow of a doubt that God has spoken.

> *Be still, and know that I am God.*
> (Psalm 46:10)

One word of caution—when trying to decipher if it was truly God who responded to us, we need to remember that God will never tell us something that is contrary to His written word, the Bible. If we are being led by a thought or an idea that we feel was inspired by our communication with God, we must be sure to compare it to scripture before acting upon it.

Sometimes, temptation may be whispered into our ear rather than God's answer or we may be driven by our own desires. If we are feeling any uncertainty or hesitation, it may be God trying to warn us or get us to slow down. Whenever we are in doubt about something, perhaps because we may not know God's word very well, seek godly counsel from those who do. And finally, when we are praying in a moment that is not life or death, God will not rush us into doing something, so please take a little time to ensure it agrees with His word before acting.

FORMULAS AND PRAYER PATTERNS

Sometimes it is hard to know what to pray about or how to pray, I get that. So, if you are still having difficulty getting started, here are some famous formulas for prayer and some prayer patterns you can follow to help get the ball rolling.

Please keep in mind, the following outlines are only provided for assistance in helping you establish your own communication link with God. These are not intended to be prayed word for word. After all, when you have a conversation with someone and you tell them what is going on in your life, you would use your own words, not somebody else's. As an outline, therefore, the following prayer patterns simply identify a main topic along with some thought-provoking sub-topics or suggestions to provide inspiration for your thinking and praying.

ACTS

A = Acknowledgment: Recognize our failures and ask for forgiveness.
C = Concern: Express our thoughts for others and their needs.
T = Thanksgiving: Demonstrate an attitude of gratitude toward God for what has already been done and in advance for what is yet to be done.
S = Scriptures for Strength: Read and pray the word of God for overcoming strength in our situations.

ARMOR OF GOD

(Ephesians 6:10–18)

Stripping Down (Hebrews 12:1)
A good soldier takes nothing unnecessary into battle, since it would only weigh them down or hinder their full ability. Likewise, we must recognize our need for God and lay aside the things that distract us from Him.

Cleansing (Psalm 51:2, 1 John 1:9)
A soldier goes through basic training to reshape both their mind and body and prepare for battle. Similarly, we ask for forgiveness and change through a deep reflection of our inner personality and qualities.

Garment of Praise (Isaiah 61:3, Romans 8:1)
To be effective in battle, you will need the proper outfit upon which everything else will adhere. Give God thanks for all He has done for us and exalt Him for who He is. In turn, praising God will enlighten our mood and inspire us.

Belt of Truth (Ephesians 6:14, Psalm 51:6)
We must recognize God's word as the proper authority in our lives and be completely honest with Him, others, and ourself even in the most private parts of ourself. This will center and stabilize us to stand effectively in the battle of everyday life.

Breastplate of Righteousness (Ephesians 6:14, Psalm 4:5, Isaiah 51:7, Isaiah 54:14, Romans 10:10)
Righteousness will cover our heart when we allow God to enter and rule upon the throne of our

emotions. We must trust in God whole-heartedly in every situation we face. Let Him provide protection by living according to His word.

Good-News Shoes (Ephesians 6:15, 1 Samuel 2:9, Psalm 119:105, Isaiah 52:7)
We are compelled by love to take what we have learned and share with others how we have been affected by God's word so that they, too, can come to know the God of all glory.

Shield of Faith (Ephesians 6:16, Luke 17:6 & 19, Romans 10:17, 1 Corinthians 2:5)
The battle is God's, not ours. Therefore, to snuff out every fiery dart of the enemy, we must exercise or lift up our faith. We must trust God and not lean on our own understanding. We must also link up with other believers to ensure even greater protection.

Helmet of Salvation (Ephesians 6:17, Philippians 4:7, Romans 12:2)
We must have our minds and thoughts purified and stayed on Him. We must surrender to the mind of Christ because this is the fiercest battleground. Therefore, we must diligently protect it and let God rule over it.

Sword of the Spirit (Ephesians 6:17, Hebrews 4:12, Revelation 1:16, Revelation 19:15, Proverbs 27:17)
This is the only offensive weapon and must be used with great skill and care, as it is double edged and can cut both ways. We gain a greater hold of the sword through prayer and obtain greater thrust or application of it through fasting. We stay sharp through the interaction of others, whereby we must reevaluate if we are living it or merely proclaiming it.

Cloak of Love (1 John 3:18, 1 John 4:12)
As the outer wrapping, the cloak is our final level of protection. Everything we do must be under the motivation of love—love for God, others, and even ourself.

Standing Firm in the Battle (Ephesians 6:13, Galatians 6:9, Romans 8:28)
When we are weary in well doing, we must remember that we do not operate in our strength, and we do not need to figure everything out at once. All we need to do is stand firm, unmovable in our belief that God is working all things for good.

A Final Reminder (2 Timothy 2:3–4)
We must remember that while we live in this world, we are not actually a part of it. The moment we have committed our way unto God, we become citizens of heaven and God fills us with His Spirit. Therefore, our ultimate goal is to please Him through our thoughts, words, and actions.

THE TABERNACLE PATTERN

Moving into the Camp of the Israelites (Responding to the Invitation)

First, we must possess a willingness to draw close to God and leave this world behind. We begin by moving into the camp to get nearer to the source. In other words, we respond to the invitation and associate with other believers. This is the time to thank God for the effect of others on building our faith.

Opening the First Curtain (Opening Our Heart)

This is the only way into the tabernacle. We must decide for ourself to seek God and open our heart to let Him in. Use this time to pray for understanding of His word and ask Him to provide revelation.

Stepping over the Threshold (Making Our Decision for Christ)

We all must reach the place of making a commitment to and for Christ. Each day, we are asked to put our faith into action and that commitment must be renewed.

The Altar of Sacrifice (The Cross)

We must lay down our will and repent of our sins. We must acknowledge the place that Jesus took for our punishment and realize the incredible value of his sacrifice so we could live an abundant life.

Crown of Thorns

Jesus wore this painful crown for the healing of our minds. Therefore, it is important that we learn to possess the mind of Christ.

Spitting and Buffeting

Jesus suffered this brutality to show us what true humility is and to provide for the healing of our emotions. Therefore, we must no longer be ruled by what we feel, being tossed about by every wave of emotion, and instead trust and rely on what we know in God's word.

Scourged Back

Our Savior accepted this punishment to release physical healing to us and to lighten our loads.

Nails in Hands

This cruelty provided our redemption from the slavery of sin. Now we are equipped to do the work of God.

Nails in Feet

This malice toward the King of Peace bought us redemption from impure desires. Now we are enabled to walk in the will of God.

Spear-Pierced Side

This act of torture provided a great exposure for us to receive and give godly love.

Nakedness and Death

Jesus accepted this humility so we could live by his perfect example. We are reminded to die to our self-will daily.

The Laver of Water (Baptism)

This process of washing should cause inner reflection of our mind, body, and spirit. Specifically, it should point us toward lining our life up to God's word, as summed up in His Ten Commandments.

1. No Other Gods

2. No Idols

3. Do Not Use God's Name in Vain

4. Keep the Sabbath Holy

5. Honor Your Mother and Father

6. Do Not Kill

7. Do Not Commit Adultery

8. Do Not Steal

9. Do Not Bear False Witness

10. Do Not Covet

Opening the Second Curtain to Enter the Holy Place (Opening Our Mind to the Holy Spirit)

This begins a deeper relationship with God as the introduction to the operation of the Holy Spirit in our life. This is not for the casual observer. It's only for those who want as much of God in their life as they can get.

The Candlestick (The Illumination of the Holy Spirit Through Our Actions)

Jesus has called us to be the light of the world. In order to illuminate God's truth, we must understand God's Spirit. There are seven aspects to consider according to scripture. (Revelation 3:1, Isaiah 11:2)

1. Fear of the Lord (Respect) (Proverbs 1:7, Psalm 25:14)

2. The Spirit of the Lord (Dependence upon God) (Isaiah 59:19, 2 Corinthians 3:17)

3. Counsel (Decision-Making) (Isaiah 30:1)

4. Understanding (Direction for the Future) (Job 32:8, Proverbs 17:27)

5. Knowledge (What to Do) (Ecclesiastes 2:26)

6. Wisdom (How to Do) (Exodus 28:3, Ephesians 1:17)

7. Might (Power for Service) (Micha 3:8, 1 Corinthians 2:4)

The Table of Shewbread (the Sustenance of the Holy Spirit Through Our Relationships and the Word of God)

Jesus has come as the bread of life. Because bread supplies sustenance and life, it implies that a relationship is required. We break bread with those who are closest to us. Pray for God to sustain those relationships.

1. Spouse

2. Family (Children, Parents, Etc.)

3. Friends

4. Coworkers

5. Pastor

6. Disciples

7. God

The Altar of Incense (the Communication of the Holy Spirit Through Prayer and Worship)

God told us that He will meet our needs in prayer. The rising incense indicated the prayers of His people, made up of our various needs. God has shown Himself to be the provider of each need in a great manner of ways.

1. Jehovah Rohi (My Shepherd)

2. Jehovah Jireh (My Provider)

3. Jehovah Shalom (My Peace)

4. Jehovah Rapha (My Healer)

5. Jehovah Tsidkenu (My Righteousness)

6. Jehovah Shammah (My Presence)

7. Jehovah Nissi (My Defender)

The Last Curtain (The Veil of Jesus's Flesh)
We are to circumcise our heart rather than our flesh. The sacrifice for our sins was made once and for all.

1. **The Sacrifice** (Hebrews 10:20)

2. **Circumcise our Heart** (Romans 2:29)

Stepping Into the Holy of Holies (The Infilling of the Holy Spirit)
It is in this setting that we dive into such a deep personal relationship with God where we commune on a level that only together we can comprehend.

1. **Teaches Us** (Luke 12:12, 1 Corinthians 2:13)

2. **Brings to Our Remembrance** (John 14:26)

3. **Power to Witness** (Acts 1:8)

4. **Righteousness, Peace, and Joy** (Romans 14:1, Romans 15:13)

Ark of the Covenant and the Mercy Seat (Intercession for Others)
Through His mercy, we can come boldly to God and ask not only for our needs but also for the needs of others.

1. **Intercession** (Hebrews 4:16)
   a. Prayer for Others (Global, National, State, and City Authorities, and the Lost)
   b. Petition (Needs of Others)
   c. Thankfulness on Their Behalf

The Law of God (Love)
Since God is love and He demonstrated that love for us, we should be willing to love as well. Therefore, we should ask God to teach us to love perfectly.

1. **God is Love** (Romans 5:5, Romans 8:38–39, 1 John 4:8)

2. **God Loves Us** (John 3:16, 1 John 4:9–10 & 16 & 19)

3. **We Must Demonstrate God's Love** (Deuteronomy 10:12, Mark 12:30, 1 John 2:5, 1 John 4:7 & 11–18 & 20–21, 1 John 5:1–3)

Back Out into the World
We are to take the gospel back out to others.

1. Proverbs 11:30

2. Isaiah 52:7

3. Romans 10:15

4. Matthew 9:36–38

THE LORD'S PRAYER

This beautiful prayer in poetry form is simply intended to be an outline to inspire our thoughts as we pray to God. While it may be good on occasion to say this prayer just as it's given in scripture, it is even better if we capitalize upon the ideas of each phrase and reframe it into our own words. It's important to note for prayer to come from our heart, we must put it into our own words. I have separated the phrases to emphasize ideas we can reflect on and pray about.

Our Father
which art in heaven,
Hallowed be thy name.
Thy kingdom come.
Thy will be done in earth, as it is in heaven.
Give us this day our daily bread.
And forgive us our debts,
as we forgive our debtors.
And lead us not into temptation,
but deliver us from evil:
For thine is the kingdom,
and the power,
and the glory, forever,
Amen.
(Matthew 6:9–13)

THE PRAYER CLOCK

Spending just five minutes on each of the following sections will move you quickly through an hour of prayer. If you're not ready for a full hour, start small with a simple thirty seconds on each for a total of six minutes, then move up to a minute on each for a total of twelve minutes, and continue to grow into a full hour of prayer.

1. **Praise** (Hebrews 13:15)
   Begin all prayer with praise, esteeming God for His greatness. Whatever our ultimate goal may be, always begin by praising God!

2. **Forgiveness** (Matthew 6:14–15)
   Nothing will block our spiritual growth more than an unforgiving spirit. Even a small root of bitterness will quickly grow into a serious problem. Therefore, completely pour out any feelings that might have developed against anyone.

3. **Confession** (Psalm 139:23–24)
   Early in prayer we must deal with sin. If we hide sin in our heart, God will not hear us. Ridding ourself of sin will clear the road for powerful prayer.

4. **Petition** (James 4:2–3, Matthew 6:9–13, 1 Peter 5:7)
   This aspect of prayer deals with our personal needs. Take them to the Lord and leave them there. Cast all your cares upon Him.

5. **Intercession** (Matthew 9:37–38, 1 Timothy 2:1–2)
   Intercession is a deep-felt prayer for the needs of others. It involves the most intense dimension of prayer and is God's love flowing through us.

6. **Read the Word** (2 Timothy 3:16)
It may surprise some to hear the suggestion that we should read our Bible during prayer. However, His word enlightens the eyes. When we read the Bible, new possibilities are revealed.

7. **Meditation** (Psalm 1:1–2, Psalm 77:12)
Take time to think on the things of God. He will open your understanding through this process.

8. **Thanksgiving** (Philippians 4:6)
Although we will probably do this throughout our prayer time, we must make sure we spend a special dedicated time thanking God for His provision and goodness to us.

9. **Pray the Word** (Romans 10:8, Hebrews 4:12)
Faith is in our mouth, so express it. It is also quick, powerful, and sharp, so use it to change situations for the better.

10. **Singing** (Psalm 100:2)
Singing refreshes and comforts the soul. Try singing in the Spirit!

11. **Listening** (1 Kings 19:11–12, Deuteronomy 28:2)
Prayer is not all about talking *to* God. It also involves *listening* for directions *from* God. Try to train your ear to hear His still, small voice. Remember, His spoken word will always line up with His written word, the Bible.

12. **Praise** (Psalm 34:1)
Conclude every prayer with praise and worship. We exalt the nature of God and praise Him simply for who He is.

THE PRAYER OF JABEZ

This short prayer can also act as an outline to stir our thoughts as we talk to God from our heart. Like the Lord's Prayer, it may be good to say this prayer as presented in scripture at times, however it's usually better if we can put it into our own words, emphasizing the ideas Jabez expressed.

> *Oh that thou wouldest bless me indeed,*
> *and enlarge my coast,*
> *and that thine hand might be with me,*
> *and that thou wouldest keep me from evil,*
> *that it may not grieve me!*
> (1 Chronicles 4:10)

OTHER PRAYERS IN SCRIPTURE

There are a multitude of prayers made throughout scripture that can be used as a basis or model for our own prayers. Again, the key is rephrasing them into our own words where or whenever possible. Seek to relate to the concept or main idea of the prayer and how it may parallel our own life and situation. Here are just a few for reference. Use the notes section in this journal to identify any you find in scripture that inspire you to pray.

1. **Abraham's Negotiation** (Genesis 18:17–33)
2. **Jacob's Wrestling** (Genesis 32:9–12)
3. **Hannah's Request** (1 Samuel 1:1–18)
4. **Solomon's Wisdom** (1 Kings 3:1–15)
5. **Job's Confession** (Job 42:1–6)
6. **David's Repentance** (Psalm 51:1–19)
7. **Jonah's Cry** (Jonah 2:1–10)
8. **Jesus's Prayer for Unity** (John 17:1–26)
9. **Acts of Boldness** (Acts 4:1–31)

PRAYING IN THE SPIRIT

Ask God for understanding and the blessing of this gift.

The Benefits
Ask God to help you see and comprehend.

1. **Understanding God's Word** (Luke 12:12, 1 Corinthians 2:13, John 14:26)
2. **Building Up Faith** (Jude 1:20)
3. **Joy Unspeakable** (Romans 14:17, Romans 15:13)
4. **Power to Witness** (Acts 1:8)

The Fruit (Galatians 5:22–23)
Consider areas you may need God to help develop, or how they could apply to situations you are facing.

1. **Love** (1 Corinthians 13:1–13)
2. **Joy** (Romans 5:11, Romans 15:13)
3. **Peace** (Romans 5:1, Romans 8:6, Philippians 4:7, Hebrews 12:14)
4. **Longsuffering/Forbearance/Patience** (Ephesians 4:2, Colossians 3:12, 2 Peter 3:9)
5. **Gentleness/Kindness** (Psalm 18:35)
6. **Goodness** (Romans 11:22, Psalm 23:6, Psalm 31:19)
7. **Faith** (Romans 1:17, Romans 5:1, Romans 10:8, Romans 10:17)
8. **Meekness/Humility/Modesty** (Galatians 6:1, Ephesians 4:2, 1 Peter 3:15)
9. **Temperance/Self-Control** (2 Peter 1:5–7)

The Gifts (1 Corinthians 12:1–11)
Seek that God would use us to deliver the right gift to the right person at the right time. Ask how

they may be applied to our current situations and relationships.

1. **Wisdom** (Romans 11:33, 1 Corinthians 2:6–7, Colossians 3:16, James 1:5, James 3:17)
2. **Knowledge** (Romans 3:20, 11:33, 1 Corinthians 1:5, Philippians 1:9, Philippians 3:8)
3. **Faith** (Romans 1:17, Romans 3:27–28, Romans 5:1–2, Galatians 3:26, Ephesians 2:8, 1 Timothy 6:12, Hebrews 4:2, Hebrews 11:1, Hebrews 11:6)
4. **Healings** (Matthew 4:23, Matthew 9:35, Luke 9:6 & 11)
5. **Miracles and Wonders** (John 2:23, John 7:31, Acts 2:43, Acts 5:12, Acts 6:8, Acts 7:36, Acts 8:6, Acts 15:12, Acts 19:11)
6. **Prophecy** (Romans 12:6, 2 Peter 1:19)
7. **Discernment** (Nehemiah 8:8, Hebrews 5:14)
8. **Diverse Tongues** (Mark 16:17, Acts 2:4, 1 Corinthians 13:1, 1 Corinthians 14:5 & 22 & 39)
9. **Interpretation** (1 Corinthians 14:26, 2 Peter 1:20)

FAVORITE PSALMS

Spend time praying through the psalms. Psalms is a unique book in the Bible in that it consists solely of prayers and songs. In fact, the word "psalm" means a sacred song.

The book of Psalms expresses a wide range of human emotions, and we can almost always find one to fit whatever we are feeling at any given moment. Using these psalms, we will have a starting point to express ourself to God. In addition, we will begin to develop a few favorites of our own that we may want to refer to again and again (you can write them down in the notes section of this prayer journal). Some of my personal favorites include:

1. **Dealing with Difficult People** (Psalm 3)
2. **Trusting God's Word** (Psalm 19)
3. **Peace and Comfort** (Psalm 23)
4. **Strength and Encouragement** (Psalm 27)
5. **Finding Refreshment** (Psalm 32)
6. **Praising the Lord** (Psalm 33, Psalm 100, Psalm 150)
7. **Understanding God's Goodness** (Psalm 34)
8. **Expressing Our Desires to God** (Psalm 37)
9. **Trusting God to Come Through** (Psalm 46)
10. **Repentance** (Psalm 52)
11. **Release of Burdens** (Psalm 55)
12. **Hope** (Psalm 71)
13. **Protection** (Psalm 91)
14. **Appreciation of God's Word** (Psalm 119)

FAVORITE PROVERBS

In addition to the book of Psalms, the book of Proverbs can open our eyes to aspects of prayer as well. A proverb is a short lesson-heavy story or poem.

Spending time praying through the proverbs will show us areas in which we may need greater wisdom and practice. We may also find one that provides the answers we are looking for in that moment. (Write your favorites down in the notes section of this prayer journal!) Here are some of the ones that move me:

1. **Trusting in God and His Benefits** (Proverbs 3)
2. **Wisdom** (Proverbs 4)
3. **God's Instruction** (Proverbs 8)
4. **God's Provision** (Proverbs 10)
5. **Dealing with Pride** (Proverbs 13)
6. **Relationships** (Proverbs 15)
7. **Watching Our Words** (Proverbs 18)
8. **Raising Children** (Proverbs 22)
9. **Using Our Resources** (Proverbs 25)
10. **Being Faithful** (Proverbs 28)
11. **An Example of a Virtuous Woman** (Proverbs 31)

A FEW OF GOD'S PROMISES

As we read scripture, we will notice that God has made numerous promises to those who trust in Him. A few of God's promises have been listed below as encouragement and ideas of what to pray about. Keep in mind that promises are two sided—that means if we do our part, God is bound to do His. Therefore, as you pray, ask God to help you fulfill your part and remind Him to fulfill His part. You may also want to jot down any specific promises you discover for yourself while reading the Bible.

1. **Promise of the Holy Spirit Infilling** (Luke 24:49, Acts 1:4, Acts 2:1–40)
2. **The Lord Will Fight for You** (Joshua 23:9–11)
3. **To Live a Long Life** (Ephesians 6:1–3)
4. **Reward from God** (Hebrews 10:35–37)
5. **A Crown** (James 1:12)
6. **Eternal Life** (1 John 2:24–25)

SOME PRAYER REMINDERS

There are many aspects and people who could benefit from our prayers. The list below will provide a starting point with some reminders of what we can include in our prayer time. It's a good idea to write down any other prayer reminders we like that will help us during our prayer time.

1. Leadership (Country, National, State, County)
2. Community (Schools, Neighbors, Businesses)
3. Friends
4. Family
5. Health

6. Finances

7. Ministries

8. Peace in Jerusalem and Around the World

9. Missionaries and Laborers to Spread the Gospel

10. Christ's Return

ANSWERED PRAYER

Think about your previously answered prayers, especially those that were not answered in the way you expected. The answers to our prayers often lead to new developments in our lives. Remember to thank God for His provision and use these past prayers to build new or related prayers. Things may arise that we didn't think of the first time we prayed, or situations may change as a result of our original prayer. These new events may help us focus our prayers in more meaningful ways now that we have started receiving and recognizing the answers.

One prayer may not be enough, even if your prayer was answered. For example, when we pray about someone receiving Christ, they may respond by committing their life to God. But now they will need prayer to stay the course and get proper discipleship. Yet again, here is another application of the phrase "pray without ceasing."

CLOSING THOUGHTS

As we close out this short study on prayer, I simply want to encourage you to pray! Communicate with God throughout your day. As you go about your work or when you're driving along, express your gratitude and love for God with a simple "I love you, Jesus" or a "Thank you for your goodness, God," and as you do this, quietly listen for a moment to see if God has something to say to you in return as a part of your quick exchange. I believe you will be surprised with how these spontaneous moments can bring valuable enrichment to your relationship with our Savior.

If you are looking for more resources regarding prayer, I highly recommend *Prayer* by Verbal Bean. Although it is an older book, it is still very relevant. If you need to talk to someone about your prayer life, please reach out to your pastor and make sure that what they have to say about prayer is in alignment with the Bible, which of course is the ultimate source regarding prayer. Additionally, there are numerous websites, magazines, podcasts, and other resources you can Google about prayer or the Christian life. Please be discerning and, again, use your Bible as a validator to what you read or hear. Nothing you receive should ever contradict God's word.

And of course, feel free to contact me directly at

Rick-Stephenson@wisdomwell.guru.

Thanks for reading, and may God meet you in your times of prayer. May you also find that you can express yourself to Him anytime, anywhere, and anyhow!

God Bless,

Pastor Rick

PERSONAL REFLECTIONS REGARDING PRAYER

PERSONAL REFLECTIONS REGARDING PRAYER

PERSONAL REFLECTIONS REGARDING PRAYER

PERSONAL REFLECTIONS REGARDING PRAYER

PERSONAL REFLECTIONS REGARDING PRAYER

PERSONAL REFLECTIONS REGARDING PRAYER

PERSONAL REFLECTIONS REGARDING PRAYER

PERSONAL REFLECTIONS REGARDING PRAYER

PREPARATION

Date:		Day:	Time Spent in Prayer:		Place or Setting:	
Music		Lights			Bible	
On	Off	None	Soft	Bright	On Hand	Not Available

COMMUNICATE

People Prayed For

Situations Prayed About

Personal Requests

Scriptures Prayed

FEAR NOT

After these things the word of the LORD came unto Abram in a vision, saying,
Fear not, Abram: I am thy shield, and thy exceeding great reward.
(Genesis 15:1)

BASICS

Who Prayed
With Me:

Prayer Pattern
Used:

LISTEN

Things God Spoke Directly to Me Through Dreams or a Word of Prophecy

Scriptures That Came to Mind

Answers or Other Experiences That Demonstrated God to Me

Reminders and Notes

REJOICE

And there ye shall eat before the LORD your God, and ye shall rejoice in all that ye put your
hand unto, ye and your households, wherein the LORD thy God hath blessed thee.
(Deuteronomy 12:7)

PREPARATION

Date:		Day:	Time Spent in Prayer:		Place or Setting:	
Music		Lights			Bible	
On	Off	None	Soft	Bright	On Hand	Not Available

COMMUNICATE

People Prayed For

Situations Prayed About

Personal Requests

Scriptures Prayed

FEAR NOT

And God heard the voice of the lad; and the angel of God called to Hagar out of heaven,
and said unto her, What aileth thee, Hagar fear not;
for God hath heard the voice of the lad where he is.
(Genesis 21:17)

BASICS

Who Prayed
With Me:

Prayer Pattern
Used:

LISTEN

Things God Spoke Directly to Me Through Dreams or a Word of Prophecy

Scriptures That Came to Mind

Answers or Other Experiences That Demonstrated God to Me

Reminders and Notes

REJOICE

And thou shalt rejoice before the LORD thy God, thou, and thy son, and thy daughter, and thy manservant, and thy maidservant, and the Levite that is within thy gates, and the stranger, and the fatherless, and the widow, that are among you, in the place which the LORD thy God hath chosen to place his name there.

(Deuteronomy 16:11)

PREPARATION

Date:		Day:	Time Spent in Prayer:		Place or Setting:	
Music		Lights			Bible	
On	Off	None	Soft	Bright	On Hand	Not Available

COMMUNICATE

People Prayed For

Situations Prayed About

Personal Requests

Scriptures Prayed

FEAR NOT

And the LORD appeared unto him the same night, and said, I am the God of Abraham
thy father: fear not, for I am with thee, and will bless thee,
and multiply thy seed for my servant Abraham's sake.
(Genesis 26:24)

BASICS

Who Prayed
With Me:

Prayer Pattern
Used:

LISTEN

Things God Spoke Directly to Me Through Dreams or a Word of Prophecy

Scriptures That Came to Mind

Answers or Other Experiences That Demonstrated God to Me

Reminders and Notes

REJOICE

And thou shalt rejoice in thy feast, thou, and thy son, and thy daughter, and thy manservant,
and thy maidservant, and the Levite, the stranger, and the fatherless, and the widow,
that are within thy gates.
(Deuteronomy 16:14)

PREPARATION

Date:		Day:	Time Spent in Prayer:		Place or Setting:	
Music		Lights			Bible	
On	Off	None	Soft	Bright	On Hand	Not Available

COMMUNICATE

People Prayed For

Situations Prayed About

Personal Requests

Scriptures Prayed

FEAR NOT

Now therefore fear ye not: I will nourish you, and your little ones.
And he comforted them, and spake kindly unto them.
(Genesis 50:21)

BASICS

Who Prayed
With Me:

Prayer Pattern
Used:

LISTEN

Things God Spoke Directly to Me Through Dreams or a Word of Prophecy

Scriptures That Came to Mind

Answers or Other Experiences That Demonstrated God to Me

Reminders and Notes

REJOICE

Seven days shalt thou keep a solemn feast unto the LORD thy God in the place which the LORD shall choose: because the LORD thy God shall bless thee in all thine increase, and in all the works of thine hands, therefore thou shalt surely rejoice.

(Deuteronomy 16:15)

PREPARATION

Date:		Day:	Time Spent in Prayer:		Place or Setting:	
Music		Lights			Bible	
On	Off	None	Soft	Bright	On Hand	Not Available

COMMUNICATE

People Prayed For

Situations Prayed About

Personal Requests

Scriptures Prayed

FEAR NOT

And Moses said unto the people, Fear ye not, stand still, and see the salvation of the LORD,
which he will shew to you to day: for the Egyptians whom ye have seen to day,
ye shall see them again no more for ever.

(Exodus 14:13)

BASICS

**Who Prayed
With Me:**

**Prayer Pattern
Used:**

LISTEN

Things God Spoke Directly to Me Through Dreams or a Word of Prophecy

Scriptures That Came to Mind

Answers or Other Experiences That Demonstrated God to Me

Reminders and Notes

REJOICE

*And thou shalt rejoice in every good thing which the LORD thy God hath given unto thee,
and unto thine house, thou, and the Levite, and the stranger that is among you.*

(Deuteronomy 26:11)

PREPARATION

Date:		Day:	Time Spent in Prayer:		Place or Setting:	
Music		Lights			Bible	
On	Off	None	Soft	Bright	On Hand	Not Available

COMMUNICATE

People Prayed For

Situations Prayed About

Personal Requests

Scriptures Prayed

FEAR NOT

And Moses said unto the people, Fear not: for God is come to prove you,
and that his fear may be before your faces, that ye sin not.
(Exodus 20:20)

BASICS

Who Prayed
With Me:

Prayer Pattern
Used:

LISTEN

Things God Spoke Directly to Me Through Dreams or a Word of Prophecy

Scriptures That Came to Mind

Answers or Other Experiences That Demonstrated God to Me

Reminders and Notes

REJOICE

Rejoice, O ye nations, with his people: for he will avenge the blood of his servants, and will render vengeance to his adversaries, and will be merciful unto his land, and to his people.

(Deuteronomy 32:43)

PREPARATION

Date:		Day:	Time Spent in Prayer:		Place or Setting:	
Music		Lights			Bible	
On	Off	None	Soft	Bright	On Hand	Not Available

COMMUNICATE

People Prayed For

Situations Prayed About

Personal Requests

Scriptures Prayed

FEAR NOT

Only rebel not ye against the LORD, neither fear ye the people of the land;
for they are bread for us: their defence is departed from them, and the LORD
is with us: fear them not.

(Numbers 14:9)

BASICS

Who Prayed
With Me:

Prayer Pattern
Used:

LISTEN

Things God Spoke Directly to Me Through Dreams or a Word of Prophecy

Scriptures That Came to Mind

Answers or Other Experiences That Demonstrated God to Me

Reminders and Notes

REJOICE

*And Hannah prayed, and said, My heart rejoiceth in the LORD, mine horn is
exalted in the LORD: my mouth is enlarged over mine enemies; because I rejoice in thy salvation.*
(1 Samuel 2:1)

PREPARATION

Date:		Day:	Time Spent in Prayer:		Place or Setting:	
Music		Lights			Bible	
On	Off	None	Soft	Bright	On Hand	Not Available

COMMUNICATE

People Prayed For

Situations Prayed About

Personal Requests

Scriptures Prayed

FEAR NOT

Behold, the LORD thy God hath set the land before thee: go up and possess it,
as the LORD God of thy fathers hath said unto thee; fear not, neither be discouraged.

(Deuteronomy 1:21)

BASICS

Who Prayed
With Me:

Prayer Pattern
Used:

LISTEN

Things God Spoke Directly to Me Through Dreams or a Word of Prophecy

Scriptures That Came to Mind

Answers or Other Experiences That Demonstrated God to Me

Reminders and Notes

REJOICE

Glory ye in his holy name: let the heart of them rejoice that seek the LORD.
(1 Chronicles 16:10)

PREPARATION

Date:		Day:	Time Spent in Prayer:		Place or Setting:	
Music		Lights			Bible	
On	Off	None	Soft	Bright	On Hand	Not Available

COMMUNICATE

People Prayed For

Situations Prayed About

Personal Requests

Scriptures Prayed

FEAR NOT

Ye shall not fear them: for the LORD your God he shall fight for you.
(Deuteronomy 3:22)

BASICS

Who Prayed
With Me:

Prayer Pattern
Used:

LISTEN

Things God Spoke Directly to Me Through Dreams or a Word of Prophecy

Scriptures That Came to Mind

Answers or Other Experiences That Demonstrated God to Me

Reminders and Notes

REJOICE

Let the heavens be glad, and let the earth rejoice:
and let men say among the nations,
The LORD reigneth.
(1 Chronicles 16:31)

PREPARATION

Date:		Day:	Time Spent in Prayer:		Place or Setting:	
Music		Lights			Bible	
On	Off	None	Soft	Bright	On Hand	Not Available

COMMUNICATE

People Prayed For

Situations Prayed About

Personal Requests

Scriptures Prayed

FEAR NOT

Be strong and of a good courage, fear not, nor be afraid of them: for the LORD thy God,
he it is that doth go with thee; he will not fail thee, nor forsake thee.
(Deuteronomy 31:6)

BASICS

Who Prayed
With Me:

Prayer Pattern
Used:

LISTEN

Things God Spoke Directly to Me Through Dreams or a Word of Prophecy

Scriptures That Came to Mind

Answers or Other Experiences That Demonstrated God to Me

Reminders and Notes

REJOICE

Serve the LORD with fear, and rejoice with trembling.
(Psalm 2:11)

PREPARATION

Date:		Day:	Time Spent in Prayer:		Place or Setting:	
Music		Lights			Bible	
On	Off	None	Soft	Bright	On Hand	Not Available

COMMUNICATE

People Prayed For

Situations Prayed About

Personal Requests

Scriptures Prayed

FEAR NOT

And he answered, Fear not: for they that be with us are more than they that be with them.

(2 Kings 6:16)

BASICS

Who Prayed
With Me:

Prayer Pattern
Used:

LISTEN

Things God Spoke Directly to Me Through Dreams or a Word of Prophecy

Scriptures That Came to Mind

Answers or Other Experiences That Demonstrated God to Me

Reminders and Notes

REJOICE

But let all those that put their trust in thee rejoice: let them ever shout for joy,
because thou defendest them: let them also that love thy name be joyful in thee.
(Psalm 5:11)

PREPARATION

Date:		Day:	Time Spent in Prayer:		Place or Setting:	
Music		Lights			Bible	
On	Off	None	Soft	Bright	On Hand	Not Available

COMMUNICATE

People Prayed For

Situations Prayed About

Personal Requests

Scriptures Prayed

FEAR NOT

And David said to Solomon his son, Be strong and of good courage, and do it: fear not, nor be dismayed: for the LORD God, even my God, will be with thee; he will not fail thee, nor forsake thee, until thou hast finished all the work for the service of the house of the LORD.

(1 Chronicles 28:20)

BASICS

Who Prayed
With Me:

Prayer Pattern
Used:

LISTEN

Things God Spoke Directly to Me Through Dreams or a Word of Prophecy

Scriptures That Came to Mind

Answers or Other Experiences That Demonstrated God to Me

Reminders and Notes

REJOICE

I will be glad and rejoice in thee: I will sing praise to thy name, O thou most High.

(Psalm 9:2)

PREPARATION

Date:		Day:	Time Spent in Prayer:		Place or Setting:	
Music		Lights			Bible	
On	Off	None	Soft	Bright	On Hand	Not Available

COMMUNICATE

People Prayed For

Situations Prayed About

Personal Requests

Scriptures Prayed

FEAR NOT

Ye shall not need to fight in this battle: set yourselves, stand ye still, and see the salvation of the LORD with you, O Judah and Jerusalem: fear not, nor be dismayed; to morrow go out against them: for the LORD will be with you.

(2 Chronicles 20:17)

BASICS

Who Prayed
With Me:

Prayer Pattern
Used:

LISTEN

Things God Spoke Directly to Me Through Dreams or a Word of Prophecy

Scriptures That Came to Mind

Answers or Other Experiences That Demonstrated God to Me

Reminders and Notes

REJOICE

That I may shew forth all thy praise in the gates of the daughter of Zion:
I will rejoice in thy salvation.
(Psalm 9:14)

PREPARATION

Date:		Day:	Time Spent in Prayer:		Place or Setting:	
Music		Lights			Bible	
On	Off	None	Soft	Bright	On Hand	Not Available

COMMUNICATE

People Prayed For

Situations Prayed About

Personal Requests

Scriptures Prayed

FEAR NOT

Though an host should encamp against me, my heart shall not fear: though war should rise against me,
in this will I be confident. One thing have I desired of the LORD,
that will I seek after; that I may dwell in the house of the LORD all the days of my life,
to behold the beauty of the LORD, and to enquire in his temple.

(Psalm 27:3–4)

BASICS

Who Prayed
With Me:

Prayer Pattern
Used:

LISTEN

Things God Spoke Directly to Me Through Dreams or a Word of Prophecy

Scriptures That Came to Mind

Answers or Other Experiences That Demonstrated God to Me

Reminders and Notes

REJOICE

But I have trusted in thy mercy; my heart shall rejoice in thy salvation.

(Psalm 13:5)

PREPARATION

Date:		Day:	Time Spent in Prayer:		Place or Setting:	
Music		Lights			Bible	
On	Off	None	Soft	Bright	On Hand	Not Available

COMMUNICATE

People Prayed For

Situations Prayed About

Personal Requests

Scriptures Prayed

FEAR NOT

God is our refuge and strength, a very present help in trouble. Therefore will not we fear, though the earth be removed, and though the mountains be carried into the midst of the sea.

(Psalm 46:1–2)

BASICS

Who Prayed With Me:

Prayer Pattern Used:

LISTEN

Things God Spoke Directly to Me Through Dreams or a Word of Prophecy

Scriptures That Came to Mind

Answers or Other Experiences That Demonstrated God to Me

Reminders and Notes

REJOICE

We will rejoice in thy salvation, and in the name of our God we will set up our banners:
the LORD fulfil all thy petitions.
(Psalm 20:5)

PREPARATION

Date:		Day:	Time Spent in Prayer:		Place or Setting:	
Music		Lights			Bible	
On	Off	None	Soft	Bright	On Hand	Not Available

COMMUNICATE

People Prayed For

Situations Prayed About

Personal Requests

Scriptures Prayed

FEAR NOT

In God I will praise his word, in God I have put my trust;
I will not fear what flesh can do unto me.

(Psalm 56:4)

BASICS

Who Prayed
With Me:

Prayer Pattern
Used:

LISTEN

Things God Spoke Directly to Me Through Dreams or a Word of Prophecy

Scriptures That Came to Mind

Answers or Other Experiences That Demonstrated God to Me

Reminders and Notes

REJOICE

I will be glad and rejoice in thy mercy: for thou hast considered my trouble;
thou hast known my soul in adversities.
(Psalm 31:7)

PREPARATION

Date:		Day:	Time Spent in Prayer:		Place or Setting:	
Music		Lights			Bible	
On	Off	None	Soft	Bright	On Hand	Not Available

COMMUNICATE

People Prayed For

Situations Prayed About

Personal Requests

Scriptures Prayed

FEAR NOT

The LORD is on my side; I will not fear: what can man do unto me?

(Psalm 118:6)

BASICS

**Who Prayed
With Me:**

**Prayer Pattern
Used:**

LISTEN

Things God Spoke Directly to Me Through Dreams or a Word of Prophecy

Scriptures That Came to Mind

Answers or Other Experiences That Demonstrated God to Me

Reminders and Notes

REJOICE

*Be glad in the LORD, and rejoice, ye righteous:
and shout for joy, all ye that are upright in heart.
(Psalm 32:11)*

PREPARATION

Date:		Day:	Time Spent in Prayer:		Place or Setting:	
Music		Lights			Bible	
On	Off	None	Soft	Bright	On Hand	Not Available

COMMUNICATE

People Prayed For

Situations Prayed About

Personal Requests

Scriptures Prayed

FEAR NOT

When thou liest down, thou shalt not be afraid: yea, thou shalt lie down, and thy sleep shall be sweet. Be not afraid of sudden fear, neither of the desolation of the wicked, when it cometh. For the LORD shall be thy confidence, and shall keep thy foot from being taken.

(Proverbs 3:24–26)

BASICS

**Who Prayed
With Me:**

**Prayer Pattern
Used:**

LISTEN

Things God Spoke Directly to Me Through Dreams or a Word of Prophecy

Scriptures That Came to Mind

Answers or Other Experiences That Demonstrated God to Me

Reminders and Notes

REJOICE

Rejoice in the LORD, O ye righteous: for praise is comely for the upright.

(Psalm 33:1)

PREPARATION

Date:		Day:	Time Spent in Prayer:		Place or Setting:	
Music		Lights			Bible	
On	Off	None	Soft	Bright	On Hand	Not Available

COMMUNICATE

People Prayed For

Situations Prayed About

Personal Requests

Scriptures Prayed

FEAR NOT

Say to them that are of a fearful heart, Be strong, fear not: behold, your God will come with vengeance, even God with a recompence; he will come and save you.

(Isaiah 35:4)

BASICS

Who Prayed
With Me:

Prayer Pattern
Used:

LISTEN

Things God Spoke Directly to Me Through Dreams or a Word of Prophecy

Scriptures That Came to Mind

Answers or Other Experiences That Demonstrated God to Me

Reminders and Notes

REJOICE

For our heart shall rejoice in him, because we have trusted in his holy name.

(Psalm 33:21)

PREPARATION

Date:		Day:	Time Spent in Prayer:		Place or Setting:	
Music		Lights			Bible	
On	Off	None	Soft	Bright	On Hand	Not Available

COMMUNICATE

People Prayed For

Situations Prayed About

Personal Requests

Scriptures Prayed

FEAR NOT

Fear thou not; for I am with thee: be not dismayed; for I am thy God: I will strengthen thee; yea, I will help thee; yea, I will uphold thee with the right hand of my righteousness.

(Isaiah 41:10)

BASICS

Who Prayed
With Me:

Prayer Pattern
Used:

LISTEN

Things God Spoke Directly to Me Through Dreams or a Word of Prophecy

Scriptures That Came to Mind

Answers or Other Experiences That Demonstrated God to Me

Reminders and Notes

REJOICE

And my soul shall be joyful in the LORD: it shall rejoice in his salvation.

(Psalm 35:9)

PREPARATION

Date:		Day:	Time Spent in Prayer:		Place or Setting:	
Music		Lights			Bible	
On	Off	None	Soft	Bright	On Hand	Not Available

COMMUNICATE

People Prayed For

Situations Prayed About

Personal Requests

Scriptures Prayed

FEAR NOT

For I the LORD thy God will hold thy right hand, saying unto thee, Fear not; I will help thee.
(Isaiah 41:13)

BASICS

Who Prayed
With Me:

Prayer Pattern
Used:

LISTEN

Things God Spoke Directly to Me Through Dreams or a Word of Prophecy

Scriptures That Came to Mind

Answers or Other Experiences That Demonstrated God to Me

Reminders and Notes

REJOICE

Let all those that seek thee rejoice and be glad in thee: let such as love thy salvation say continually,
The LORD be magnified.
(Psalm 40:16)

PREPARATION

Date:		Day:	Time Spent in Prayer:		Place or Setting:	
Music		Lights			Bible	
On	Off	None	Soft	Bright	On Hand	Not Available

COMMUNICATE

People Prayed For

Situations Prayed About

Personal Requests

Scriptures Prayed

FEAR NOT

But now thus saith the LORD that created thee, O Jacob, and he that formed thee, O Israel,
Fear not: for I have redeemed thee, I have called thee by thy name; thou art mine.

(Isaiah 43:1)

BASICS

Who Prayed
With Me:

Prayer Pattern
Used:

LISTEN

Things God Spoke Directly to Me Through Dreams or a Word of Prophecy

Scriptures That Came to Mind

Answers or Other Experiences That Demonstrated God to Me

Reminders and Notes

REJOICE

Make me to hear joy and gladness; that the bones which thou hast broken may rejoice.

(Psalm 51:8)

PREPARATION

Date:		Day:	Time Spent in Prayer:		Place or Setting:	
Music		Lights			Bible	
On	Off	None	Soft	Bright	On Hand	Not Available

COMMUNICATE

People Prayed For

Situations Prayed About

Personal Requests

Scriptures Prayed

FEAR NOT

Fear not: for I am with thee: I will bring thy seed from the east, and gather thee from the west.

(Isaiah 43:5)

BASICS

Who Prayed
With Me:

Prayer Pattern
Used:

LISTEN

Things God Spoke Directly to Me Through Dreams or a Word of Prophecy

Scriptures That Came to Mind

Answers or Other Experiences That Demonstrated God to Me

Reminders and Notes

REJOICE

Because thou hast been my help, therefore in the shadow of thy wings will I rejoice.

(Psalm 63:7)

PREPARATION

Date:		Day:	Time Spent in Prayer:		Place or Setting:	
Music		Lights			Bible	
On	Off	None	Soft	Bright	On Hand	Not Available

COMMUNICATE

People Prayed For

Situations Prayed About

Personal Requests

Scriptures Prayed

FEAR NOT

Hearken unto me, ye that know righteousness, the people in whose heart is my law;
fear ye not the reproach of men, neither be ye afraid of their revilings.

(Isaiah 51:7)

BASICS

Who Prayed
With Me:

Prayer Pattern
Used:

LISTEN

Things God Spoke Directly to Me Through Dreams or a Word of Prophecy

Scriptures That Came to Mind

Answers or Other Experiences That Demonstrated God to Me

Reminders and Notes

REJOICE

But let the righteous be glad; let them rejoice before God: yea, let them exceedingly rejoice.
(Psalm 68:3)

PREPARATION

Date:		Day:	Time Spent in Prayer:		Place or Setting:	
Music		Lights			Bible	
On	Off	None	Soft	Bright	On Hand	Not Available

COMMUNICATE

People Prayed For

Situations Prayed About

Personal Requests

Scriptures Prayed

FEAR NOT

Fear not; for thou shalt not be ashamed: neither be thou confounded;
for thou shalt not be put to shame: for thou shalt forget the shame of thy youth,
and shalt not remember the reproach of thy widowhood any more.

(Isaiah 54:4)

BASICS

Who Prayed
With Me:

Prayer Pattern
Used:

LISTEN

Things God Spoke Directly to Me Through Dreams or a Word of Prophecy

Scriptures That Came to Mind

Answers or Other Experiences That Demonstrated God to Me

Reminders and Notes

REJOICE

Sing unto God, sing praises to his name:
extol him that rideth upon the heavens by his name JAH,
and rejoice before him.
(Psalm 68:4)

PREPARATION

Date:		Day:	Time Spent in Prayer:		Place or Setting:	
Music		Lights			Bible	
On	Off	None	Soft	Bright	On Hand	Not Available

COMMUNICATE

People Prayed For

Situations Prayed About

Personal Requests

Scriptures Prayed

FEAR NOT

In righteousness shalt thou be established: thou shalt be far from oppression;
for thou shalt not fear: and from terror; for it shall not come near thee.
(Isaiah 54:14)

BASICS

Who Prayed With Me:

Prayer Pattern Used:

LISTEN

Things God Spoke Directly to Me Through Dreams or a Word of Prophecy

Scriptures That Came to Mind

Answers or Other Experiences That Demonstrated God to Me

Reminders and Notes

REJOICE

My lips shall greatly rejoice when I sing unto thee; and my soul, which thou hast redeemed.

(Psalm 71:23)

PREPARATION

Date:		Day:	Time Spent in Prayer:		Place or Setting:	
Music		Lights			Bible	
On	Off	None	Soft	Bright	On Hand	Not Available

COMMUNICATE

People Prayed For

Situations Prayed About

Personal Requests

Scriptures Prayed

FEAR NOT

Therefore fear thou not, O my servant Jacob, saith the LORD; neither be dismayed, O Israel:
for, lo, I will save thee from afar, and thy seed from the land of their captivity;
and Jacob shall return, and shall be in rest, and be quiet, and none shall make him afraid.
(Jeremiah 30:10)

BASICS

Who Prayed With Me:

Prayer Pattern Used:

LISTEN

Things God Spoke Directly to Me Through Dreams or a Word of Prophecy

Scriptures That Came to Mind

Answers or Other Experiences That Demonstrated God to Me

Reminders and Notes

REJOICE

Rejoice the soul of thy servant: for unto thee, O Lord, do I lift up my soul.
(Psalm 86:4)

PREPARATION

Date:		Day:	Time Spent in Prayer:		Place or Setting:	
Music		Lights			Bible	
On	Off	None	Soft	Bright	On Hand	Not Available

COMMUNICATE

People Prayed For

Situations Prayed About

Personal Requests

Scriptures Prayed

FEAR NOT

As an adamant harder than flint have I made thy forehead: fear them not,
neither be dismayed at their looks, though they be a rebellious house.
(Ezekiel 3:9)

BASICS

Who Prayed
With Me:

Prayer Pattern
Used:

LISTEN

Things God Spoke Directly to Me Through Dreams or a Word of Prophecy

Scriptures That Came to Mind

Answers or Other Experiences That Demonstrated God to Me

Reminders and Notes

REJOICE

In thy name shall they rejoice all the day:
and in thy righteousness shall they be exalted.
(Psalm 89:16)

PREPARATION

Date:		Day:	Time Spent in Prayer:		Place or Setting:	
Music		Lights			Bible	
On	Off	None	Soft	Bright	On Hand	Not Available

COMMUNICATE

People Prayed For

Situations Prayed About

Personal Requests

Scriptures Prayed

FEAR NOT

Then said he unto me, Fear not, Daniel:
for from the first day that thou didst set thine heart to understand,
and to chasten thyself before thy God,
thy words were heard, and I am come for thy words.

(Daniel 10:12)

BASICS

Who Prayed
With Me:

Prayer Pattern
Used:

LISTEN

Things God Spoke Directly to Me Through Dreams or a Word of Prophecy

Scriptures That Came to Mind

Answers or Other Experiences That Demonstrated God to Me

Reminders and Notes

REJOICE

O satisfy us early with thy mercy;
that we may rejoice and be glad all our days.
(Psalm 90:14)

PREPARATION

Date:		Day:	Time Spent in Prayer:		Place or Setting:	
Music		Lights			Bible	
On	Off	None	Soft	Bright	On Hand	Not Available

COMMUNICATE

People Prayed For

Situations Prayed About

Personal Requests

Scriptures Prayed

FEAR NOT

And said, O man greatly beloved, fear not: peace be unto thee, be strong, yea, be strong.
And when he had spoken unto me, I was strengthened, and said, Let my lord speak;
for thou hast strengthened me.
(Daniel 10:19)

BASICS

Who Prayed With Me:

Prayer Pattern Used:

LISTEN

Things God Spoke Directly to Me Through Dreams or a Word of Prophecy

Scriptures That Came to Mind

Answers or Other Experiences That Demonstrated God to Me

Reminders and Notes

REJOICE

The LORD reigneth; let the earth rejoice;
let the multitude of isles be glad thereof.
(Psalm 97:1)

PREPARATION

Date:		Day:	Time Spent in Prayer:		Place or Setting:	
Music		Lights			Bible	
On	Off	None	Soft	Bright	On Hand	Not Available

COMMUNICATE

People Prayed For

Situations Prayed About

Personal Requests

Scriptures Prayed

FEAR NOT

Fear not, O land; be glad and rejoice:
for the LORD will do great things.
(Joel 2:21)

BASICS

Who Prayed
With Me:

Prayer Pattern
Used:

LISTEN

Things God Spoke Directly to Me Through Dreams or a Word of Prophecy

Scriptures That Came to Mind

Answers or Other Experiences That Demonstrated God to Me

Reminders and Notes

REJOICE

Rejoice in the LORD, ye righteous; and give thanks at the remembrance of his holiness.

(Psalm 97:12)

PREPARATION

Date:		Day:	Time Spent in Prayer:		Place or Setting:	
Music		Lights			Bible	
On	Off	None	Soft	Bright	On Hand	Not Available

COMMUNICATE

People Prayed For

Situations Prayed About

Personal Requests

Scriptures Prayed

FEAR NOT

According to the word that I covenanted with you when ye came out of Egypt,
so my spirit remaineth among you: fear ye not.

(Haggai 2:5)

BASICS

**Who Prayed
With Me:**

**Prayer Pattern
Used:**

LISTEN

Things God Spoke Directly to Me Through Dreams or a Word of Prophecy

Scriptures That Came to Mind

Answers or Other Experiences That Demonstrated God to Me

Reminders and Notes

REJOICE

*Make a joyful noise unto the LORD, all the earth:
make a loud noise, and rejoice, and sing praise.
(Psalm 98:4)*

PREPARATION

Date:		Day:	Time Spent in Prayer:		Place or Setting:	
Music		Lights			Bible	
On	Off	None	Soft	Bright	On Hand	Not Available

COMMUNICATE

People Prayed For

Situations Prayed About

Personal Requests

Scriptures Prayed

FEAR NOT

And it shall come to pass, that as ye were a curse among the heathen,
O house of Judah, and house of Israel;
so will I save you, and ye shall be a blessing: fear not, but let your hands be strong.
(Zechariah 8:13)

BASICS

Who Prayed
With Me:

Prayer Pattern
Used:

LISTEN

Things God Spoke Directly to Me Through Dreams or a Word of Prophecy

Scriptures That Came to Mind

Answers or Other Experiences That Demonstrated God to Me

Reminders and Notes

REJOICE

Glory ye in his holy name: let the heart of them rejoice that seek the LORD.

(Psalm 105:3)

PREPARATION

Date:		Day:	Time Spent in Prayer:		Place or Setting:	
Music		Lights			Bible	
On	Off	None	Soft	Bright	On Hand	Not Available

COMMUNICATE

People Prayed For

Situations Prayed About

Personal Requests

Scriptures Prayed

FEAR NOT

And I will come near to you to judgment; and I will be a swift witness against the sorcerers, and against the adulterers, and against false swearers, and against those that oppress the hireling in his wages, the widow, and the fatherless, and that turn aside the stranger from his right, and fear not me, saith the LORD of hosts.

(Malachi 3:5)

BASICS

Who Prayed
With Me:

Prayer Pattern
Used:

LISTEN

Things God Spoke Directly to Me Through Dreams or a Word of Prophecy

Scriptures That Came to Mind

Answers or Other Experiences That Demonstrated God to Me

Reminders and Notes

REJOICE

This is the day which the LORD hath made;
we will rejoice and be glad in it.
(Psalm 118:24)

PREPARATION

Date:		Day:	Time Spent in Prayer:		Place or Setting:	
Music		Lights			Bible	
On	Off	None	Soft	Bright	On Hand	Not Available

COMMUNICATE

People Prayed For

Situations Prayed About

Personal Requests

Scriptures Prayed

FEAR NOT

Fear them not therefore:
for there is nothing covered, that shall not be revealed;
and hid, that shall not be known.
(Matthew 10:26)

BASICS

Who Prayed
With Me:

Prayer Pattern
Used:

LISTEN

Things God Spoke Directly to Me Through Dreams or a Word of Prophecy

Scriptures That Came to Mind

Answers or Other Experiences That Demonstrated God to Me

Reminders and Notes

REJOICE

I rejoice at thy word, as one that findeth great spoil.

(Psalm 119:162)

PREPARATION

Date:		Day:	Time Spent in Prayer:		Place or Setting:	
Music		Lights			Bible	
On	Off	None	Soft	Bright	On Hand	Not Available

COMMUNICATE

People Prayed For

Situations Prayed About

Personal Requests

Scriptures Prayed

FEAR NOT

And fear not them which kill the body, but are not able to kill the soul:
but rather fear him which is able to destroy both soul and body in hell.
(Matthew 10:28)

BASICS

Who Prayed
With Me:

Prayer Pattern
Used:

LISTEN

Things God Spoke Directly to Me Through Dreams or a Word of Prophecy

Scriptures That Came to Mind

Answers or Other Experiences That Demonstrated God to Me

Reminders and Notes

REJOICE

Rejoice not when thine enemy falleth, and let not thine heart be glad when he stumbleth.

(Proverbs 24:17)

PREPARATION

Date:		Day:	Time Spent in Prayer:		Place or Setting:	
Music		Lights			Bible	
On	Off	None	Soft	Bright	On Hand	Not Available

COMMUNICATE

People Prayed For

Situations Prayed About

Personal Requests

Scriptures Prayed

FEAR NOT

Fear ye not therefore, ye are of more value than many sparrows.

(Matthew 10:31)

BASICS

Who Prayed
With Me:

Prayer Pattern
Used:

LISTEN

Things God Spoke Directly to Me Through Dreams or a Word of Prophecy

Scriptures That Came to Mind

Answers or Other Experiences That Demonstrated God to Me

Reminders and Notes

REJOICE

Ointment and perfume rejoice the heart:
so doth the sweetness of a man's friend by hearty counsel.
(Proverbs 27:9)

PREPARATION

Date:		Day:	Time Spent in Prayer:		Place or Setting:	
Music		Lights			Bible	
On	Off	None	Soft	Bright	On Hand	Not Available

COMMUNICATE

People Prayed For

Situations Prayed About

Personal Requests

Scriptures Prayed

FEAR NOT

But the angel said unto him, Fear not, Zacharias: for thy prayer is heard;
and thy wife Elisabeth shall bear thee a son, and thou shalt call his name John.

(Luke 1:13)

BASICS

Who Prayed
With Me:

Prayer Pattern
Used:

LISTEN

Things God Spoke Directly to Me Through Dreams or a Word of Prophecy

Scriptures That Came to Mind

Answers or Other Experiences That Demonstrated God to Me

Reminders and Notes

REJOICE

When the righteous are in authority, the people rejoice:
but when the wicked beareth rule, the people mourn.
(Proverbs 29:2)

PREPARATION

Date:		Day:	Time Spent in Prayer:		Place or Setting:	
Music		Lights			Bible	
On	Off	None	Soft	Bright	On Hand	Not Available

COMMUNICATE

People Prayed For

Situations Prayed About

Personal Requests

Scriptures Prayed

FEAR NOT

And the angel said unto her, Fear not, Mary: for thou hast found favour with God.

(Luke 1:30)

BASICS

Who Prayed
With Me:

Prayer Pattern
Used:

LISTEN

Things God Spoke Directly to Me Through Dreams or a Word of Prophecy

Scriptures That Came to Mind

Answers or Other Experiences That Demonstrated God to Me

Reminders and Notes

REJOICE

Every man also to whom God hath given riches and wealth, and hath given him power to eat thereof, and to take his portion, and to rejoice in his labour; this is the gift of God.
(Ecclesiastes 5:19)

PREPARATION

Date:		Day:	Time Spent in Prayer:		Place or Setting:	
Music		Lights			Bible	
On	Off	None	Soft	Bright	On Hand	Not Available

COMMUNICATE

People Prayed For

Situations Prayed About

Personal Requests

Scriptures Prayed

FEAR NOT

And the angel said unto them, Fear not:
for, behold, I bring you good tidings of great joy,
which shall be to all people.
(Luke 2:10)

BASICS

Who Prayed
With Me:

Prayer Pattern
Used:

LISTEN

Things God Spoke Directly to Me Through Dreams or a Word of Prophecy

Scriptures That Came to Mind

Answers or Other Experiences That Demonstrated God to Me

Reminders and Notes

REJOICE

And it shall be said in that day, Lo, this is our God; we have waited for him, and he will save us:
this is the LORD; we have waited for him, we will be glad and rejoice in his salvation.
(Isaiah 25:9)

PREPARATION

Date:		Day:	Time Spent in Prayer:		Place or Setting:	
Music		Lights			Bible	
On	Off	None	Soft	Bright	On Hand	Not Available

COMMUNICATE

People Prayed For

Situations Prayed About

Personal Requests

Scriptures Prayed

FEAR NOT

And so was also James, and John, the sons of Zebedee, which were partners with Simon.
And Jesus said unto Simon, Fear not; from henceforth thou shalt catch men.
(Luke 5:10)

BASICS

Who Prayed
With Me:

Prayer Pattern
Used:

LISTEN

Things God Spoke Directly to Me Through Dreams or a Word of Prophecy

Scriptures That Came to Mind

Answers or Other Experiences That Demonstrated God to Me

Reminders and Notes

REJOICE

I will greatly rejoice in the LORD, my soul shall be joyful in my God; for he hath clothed me with the garments of salvation, he hath covered me with the robe of righteousness, as a bridegroom decketh himself with ornaments, and as a bride adorneth herself with her jewels.

(Isaiah 61:10)

PREPARATION

Date:		Day:	Time Spent in Prayer:		Place or Setting:	

Music		Lights			Bible	
On	Off	None	Soft	Bright	On Hand	Not Available

COMMUNICATE

People Prayed For

Situations Prayed About

Personal Requests

Scriptures Prayed

FEAR NOT

But when Jesus heard it, he answered him, saying, Fear not:
believe only, and she shall be made whole.

(Luke 8:50)

BASICS

Who Prayed
With Me:

Prayer Pattern
Used:

LISTEN

Things God Spoke Directly to Me Through Dreams or a Word of Prophecy

Scriptures That Came to Mind

Answers or Other Experiences That Demonstrated God to Me

Reminders and Notes

REJOICE

Fear not, O land; be glad and rejoice: for the LORD will do great things.

(Joel 2:21)

PREPARATION

Date:		Day:	Time Spent in Prayer:		Place or Setting:	
Music		Lights			Bible	
On	Off	None	Soft	Bright	On Hand	Not Available

COMMUNICATE

People Prayed For

Situations Prayed About

Personal Requests

Scriptures Prayed

FEAR NOT

But even the very hairs of your head are all numbered. Fear not therefore:

ye are of more value than many sparrows.

(Luke 12:7)

BASICS

Who Prayed
With Me:

Prayer Pattern
Used:

LISTEN

Things God Spoke Directly to Me Through Dreams or a Word of Prophecy

Scriptures That Came to Mind

Answers or Other Experiences That Demonstrated God to Me

Reminders and Notes

REJOICE

Rejoice not against me, O mine enemy:

when I fall, I shall arise; when I sit in darkness, the LORD shall be a light unto me.

(Micah 7:8)

PREPARATION

Date:		Day:	Time Spent in Prayer:		Place or Setting:	
Music		Lights			Bible	
On	Off	None	Soft	Bright	On Hand	Not Available

COMMUNICATE

People Prayed For

Situations Prayed About

Personal Requests

Scriptures Prayed

FEAR NOT

Fear not, little flock; for it is your Father's good pleasure to give you the kingdom.

(Luke 12:32)

BASICS

Who Prayed
With Me:

Prayer Pattern
Used:

LISTEN

Things God Spoke Directly to Me Through Dreams or a Word of Prophecy

Scriptures That Came to Mind

Answers or Other Experiences That Demonstrated God to Me

Reminders and Notes

REJOICE

Sing and rejoice, O daughter of Zion: for, lo, I come,
and I will dwell in the midst of thee, saith the LORD.
(Zechariah 2:10)

PREPARATION

Date:		Day:	Time Spent in Prayer:		Place or Setting:	
Music		Lights			Bible	
On	Off	None	Soft	Bright	On Hand	Not Available

COMMUNICATE

People Prayed For

Situations Prayed About

Personal Requests

Scriptures Prayed

FEAR NOT

Fear not, daughter of Sion: behold, thy King cometh, sitting on an ass's colt.

(John 12:15)

BASICS

**Who Prayed
With Me:**

**Prayer Pattern
Used:**

LISTEN

Things God Spoke Directly to Me Through Dreams or a Word of Prophecy

Scriptures That Came to Mind

Answers or Other Experiences That Demonstrated God to Me

Reminders and Notes

REJOICE

*Notwithstanding in this rejoice not, that the spirits are subject unto you;
but rather rejoice, because your names are written in heaven.*

(Luke 10:20)

PREPARATION

Date:		Day:	Time Spent in Prayer:		Place or Setting:	
Music		Lights			Bible	
On	Off	None	Soft	Bright	On Hand	Not Available

COMMUNICATE

People Prayed For

Situations Prayed About

Personal Requests

Scriptures Prayed

FEAR NOT

For ye have not received the spirit of bondage again to fear;
but ye have received the Spirit of adoption, whereby we cry, Abba, Father.
(Romans 8:15)

BASICS

Who Prayed
With Me:

Prayer Pattern
Used:

LISTEN

Things God Spoke Directly to Me Through Dreams or a Word of Prophecy

Scriptures That Came to Mind

Answers or Other Experiences That Demonstrated God to Me

Reminders and Notes

REJOICE

Rejoice with them that do rejoice, and weep with them that weep.

(Romans 12:15)

PREPARATION

Date:		Day:	Time Spent in Prayer:		Place or Setting:	
Music		Lights			Bible	
On	Off	None	Soft	Bright	On Hand	Not Available

COMMUNICATE

People Prayed For

Situations Prayed About

Personal Requests

Scriptures Prayed

FEAR NOT

For God hath not given us the spirit of fear; but of power, and of love, and of a sound mind.

(2 Timothy 1:7)

BASICS

Who Prayed
With Me:

Prayer Pattern
Used:

LISTEN

Things God Spoke Directly to Me Through Dreams or a Word of Prophecy

Scriptures That Came to Mind

Answers or Other Experiences That Demonstrated God to Me

Reminders and Notes

REJOICE

Rejoice in the Lord always: and again I say, Rejoice.

(Philippians 4:4)

PREPARATION

Date:		Day:	Time Spent in Prayer:		Place or Setting:	
Music		Lights			Bible	
On	Off	None	Soft	Bright	On Hand	Not Available

COMMUNICATE

People Prayed For

Situations Prayed About

Personal Requests

Scriptures Prayed

FEAR NOT

So that we may boldly say, The Lord is my helper,
and I will not fear what man shall do unto me.
(Hebrews 13:6)

BASICS

Who Prayed
With Me:

Prayer Pattern
Used:

LISTEN

Things God Spoke Directly to Me Through Dreams or a Word of Prophecy

Scriptures That Came to Mind

Answers or Other Experiences That Demonstrated God to Me

Reminders and Notes

REJOICE

Rejoice evermore.
(1 Thessalonians 5:16)

PREPARATION

Date:		Day:	Time Spent in Prayer:		Place or Setting:	
Music		Lights			Bible	
On	Off	None	Soft	Bright	On Hand	Not Available

COMMUNICATE

People Prayed For

Situations Prayed About

Personal Requests

Scriptures Prayed

FEAR NOT

There is no fear in love; but perfect love casteth out fear:
because fear hath torment.
He that feareth is not made perfect in love.
(1 John 4:18)

BASICS

Who Prayed
With Me:

Prayer Pattern
Used:

LISTEN

Things God Spoke Directly to Me Through Dreams or a Word of Prophecy

Scriptures That Came to Mind

Answers or Other Experiences That Demonstrated God to Me

Reminders and Notes

REJOICE

Whom having not seen, ye love; in whom, though now ye see him not,
yet believing, ye rejoice with joy unspeakable and full of glory.
(1 Peter 1:8)

PREPARATION

Date:		Day:	Time Spent in Prayer:		Place or Setting:	
Music		Lights			Bible	
On	Off	None	Soft	Bright	On Hand	Not Available

COMMUNICATE

People Prayed For

Situations Prayed About

Personal Requests

Scriptures Prayed

FEAR NOT

And when I saw him, I fell at his feet as dead. And he laid his right hand upon me,
saying unto me, Fear not; I am the first and the last.
(Revelation 1:17)

BASICS

Who Prayed With Me:

Prayer Pattern Used:

LISTEN

Things God Spoke Directly to Me Through Dreams or a Word of Prophecy

Scriptures That Came to Mind

Answers or Other Experiences That Demonstrated God to Me

Reminders and Notes

REJOICE

But rejoice, inasmuch as ye are partakers of Christ's sufferings;
that, when his glory shall be revealed, ye may be glad also with exceeding joy.
(1 Peter 4:13)

NOTES — THOUGHTS — SKETCHES AND IDEAS

NOTES — THOUGHTS — SKETCHES AND IDEAS

NOTES — THOUGHTS — SKETCHES AND IDEAS

NOTES — THOUGHTS — SKETCHES AND IDEAS

NOTES – THOUGHTS – SKETCHES AND IDEAS

NOTES — THOUGHTS — SKETCHES AND IDEAS

NOTES — THOUGHTS — SKETCHES AND IDEAS

NOTES — THOUGHTS — SKETCHES AND IDEAS

NOTES — THOUGHTS — SKETCHES AND IDEAS

NOTES — THOUGHTS — SKETCHES AND IDEAS

NOTES — THOUGHTS — SKETCHES AND IDEAS

NOTES — THOUGHTS — SKETCHES AND IDEAS

NOTES — THOUGHTS — SKETCHES AND IDEAS

NOTES — THOUGHTS — SKETCHES AND IDEAS

NOTES — THOUGHTS — SKETCHES AND IDEAS

NOTES — THOUGHTS — SKETCHES AND IDEAS

About the Author

Pastor Rick Stephenson has two grown children and lives with his beautiful wife in Johnson Creek, Wisconsin.

As a licensed minister with the Assemblies of God, Pastor Rick refers to himself as a worship evangelist, combining his musical ability with his motivational speaking talents. He travels the US to preach the gospel and enjoys seeing people be impacted by the power of God. He has witnessed numerous individuals healed and restored through his services, for which he gives all the glory to God. As a worship leader, he writes original spirit-filled contemporary Christian worship music. Pastor Rick has released four full-length albums as well as two EPs, won several songwriting awards, and received airplay in both the US and overseas.

In addition to being a minister, Pastor Rick is a certified master financial coach, experienced CPA, CMA, and real estate agent. He is also the CEO of Wisdom Well Abundance Coaching, LLC, and is passionate about helping people experience the most out of life. He teaches his clients how a spiritual center can help balance all areas of life, resulting in improved relationships, mental clarity, and greater physical health.

If you're interested in learning more about how Pastor Rick can help you in this way, visit **www.WisdomWell.guru** today!

Your Turn to Share God's Promises

Thank You for Reading My Book!

I truly appreciate all your feedback
and I love hearing what you have to say.
I need your input to make the next version
of this book and my future books better.
Please take two minutes now to leave a helpful review
letting me know what you
thought of the book:

(www.WisdomWell.guru/Review)

Thank you so much!

Pastor Rick Stephenson

What's Next?

Sign Up for Abundance Coaching!

I love working with those who are interested in pursuing the abundance of God. I provide coaching to help you on your journey from both a spiritual and practical perspective. From my background of over thirty years in finance and business and over twenty years as a licensed minister, I can provide sound advice to help you navigate the difficulties of life.

**Set up a consultation today at
https://calendly.com/rick-stephenson**

Website: www.WisdomWell.guru

I look forward to talking with you!

Pastor Rick Stephenson

www.ingramcontent.com/pod-product-compliance
Lightning Source LLC
Chambersburg PA
CBHW070704130626
46553CB00005B/1837